# TREES

............................................

# OF AUSTRALIA

Peter Krisch

First published in 2015 by Reed New Holland Publishers Pty Ltd
Sydney • Auckland

Level 1, 178 Fox Valley Road, Wahroonga, 2076, NSW, Australia
5/39 Woodside Avenue, Northcote, Auckland 0627, New Zealand

www.newhollandpublishers.com

ISBN 978 1 92151 752 5

Managing Director: Fiona Schultz
Publisher and Project Editor: Simon Papps
Designer: Thomas Casey, Andrew Davies
Production Director: Olga Dementiev
Printer: Toppan Leefung Printing Limited

10 9 8 7 6 5 4

Front cover images: Main left: Antarctic Beech *Nothofagus moorei;* Main right: Rose-leaved Marara *Ackama paniculata;* Top left: Giant Stinging Tree *Dendrocnide excelsa;* Bottom right: Curtain Fig *Ficus virens.*

Back cover images: Top to bottom: Crimson Bottlebrush *Callistemon citrinus*; Soft Tree Fern *Dicksonia antarctica*; Beach Casuarina *Casuarina equisetifolia.*

Page 1: Tall Eucalypt forest.
Page 3: Mulgrave Satinash (*Syzygium xerampelinum*).
Pages 4–5: Mount Warning National Park, New South Wales.
Pages 12–13: Mossman River Gorge, north Queensland.
Pages 18–19: Bull Kauri Pines (*Agathis microstachya*).
Pages 24-25: Grey Myrtle (*Backhousia myrtifolia*) flower.

Pages 46–47: Johnson's Grevillea (*Grevillea johnsonii*) flower.
Pages 56–57: Wattle (Acacia) flowers.
Pages 64–65: River She-oak (*Casuarina cunninghamiana*) stand.
Pages 72–73: Subtropical rainforest.
Pages 112–113: New England Wilderness, New South Wales.
Inside back flap: Subtropical rainforest.

## Photographic Acknowledgements

Andrew Williamson: Page 9, Page 17 (top right), Page 32 (top right), Page 37 (top left), Page 61 (top left), Page 70 (top); istock: Page 6 Huon Pine (bottom left); shutterstock: Page 35 Karri (bottom), Page 61 (top) Mulga Wattle.

## Acknowledgement

The author wishes to acknowledge the service and facilities that Australian National Parks and Reserves extend to those with an affinity to our unique flora and fauna. These important parks protect our diverse natural heritage and rare habitats. I also wish to commend the dedication of volunteers who manage and maintain Australia's many Botanical Gardens in regional and major cities.

## Dedication

Dedicated to the beauty, great diversity and unique evolution of Australian Forests.

Keep up with New Holland Publishers on Facebook
www.facebook.com/NewHollandPublishers

# CONTENTS

# INTRODUCTION

# An Introduction to Trees
❀

## What is a Tree or Shrub?

A tree is a woody plant living for more than two years (a perennial), which is more than 4m tall when fully grown and most often single-trunked. A shrub is a woody self-supporting plant (a perennial), which is less than 4m, but more than 1.5m tall when mature and often develops multiple stems. Trees can be reduced to shrub size under adverse conditions, and sometimes shrubs can reach the height of a small tree under ideal conditions.

## What Age can Australian Trees reach?

Shrubs are less likely to live as long as large trees. Wattle trees (Acacias) are relatively short-lived, on average only 25 years, with the exception of the Blackwood (*Acacia melanoxylon*), which in Tasmania can survive for 100 years or more. Very tall Eucalyptus 'Gum Trees' like the Flooded Gum (*Eucalyptus grandis*) in New South Wales, the Karri (*E. diversicolor*) in south Western Australia and the Mountain Ash (*E. regnans*) in Tasmania and Victoria can grow to 400 years old. Fig Trees such as the Curtain Fig (*Ficus virens*) in Queensland can reach an age of more than 1,000 years. The Kauri Pine (*Agathis robusta*) is a tall Conifer with origins dating back to the time of the Dinosaurs

Ancient Curtain Fig (*Ficus virens*).

Huon Pine
(*Lagarostrobos franklinii*).

(Jurassic) and has the incredible ability to live for more than 2,000 years. A Huon Pine (*Lagarostrobos franklinii*) growing in Tasmania is believed to be close to 4,000 years old and one of the oldest living plants in the world.

# How tall do Trees grow in Australia?

The tallest tree species in Australia is the Mountain Ash (*Eucalyptus regnans*) in Tasmania and Victoria, which can reach a height of more than 100m. Historic evidence suggests that exceptional trees logged by early settlers were up to 140m tall. After the Californian Redwoods the Mountain Ash is the second tallest plant in the world. They are closely followed by the Karri (*E. diversicolor*) from Western Australia and the Flooded Gum (*E. grandis*) in New South Wales, both able to attain heights of more than 80m. The ancient conifers and other rainforest giants with large buttress roots are often more than 50m tall.

# How are Trees categorised by Size?

| Size: | Height in metres: |
|---|---|
| Shrub | 1.5 to 4.0 |
| Small Tree | More than 4 to less than 10 |
| Medium Tree | 10 to 25 |
| Tall Tree | 25 to 45 |
| Very Tall Tree | More than 45 |

Dimensions are intended as a guide only, because it is often rather difficult to estimate the height of a tree in a forest. The term 'large tree' is used to describe a species with a wide spreading crown. For example the canopy spread of a Fig tree can reach up to 50m in diameter.

Above: Mountain Ash (*Eucalyptus regnans*).
Below: Bull Kauri Pine (*Agathis microstachya*).

# What are Forests and Woodlands?

Factors in distinguishing forest types are the height of trees forming the top canopy level (stratum) and the percentage of sunlight reaching the ground, i.e. the density of the forest canopy. In general trees in dense stands are called a forest, whereas sparse stands are called woodlands.

In a **tall closed forest** trees are more than 30m high and less than 30 per cent of sunlight reaches the ground.

In a **tall forest** trees are more than 30m high and less than 50 per cent of sunlight gets through to ground-level.

In a **tall open forest** trees are more than 30m high with 50 per cent to 70 per cent of sunlight reaching the forest floor.

Rainforests are closed forests and often feature two or three levels of vegetation (strata).

**Woodlands** are forests where more than 70 per cent of sunlight penetrates the canopy.

# How are Forests distributed in Australia?

The main factors for the distribution of forests are: the annual rainfall total, climatic conditions, geographical location and soil types. The arid inland regions, receiving less than 250mm of yearly rainfall, are the home to tall shrubs of the Wattle (Acacia) family known as Mulga or Myall (scrub) in Western Australia. A Mallee is low open woodland dominated by small eucalyptus species and occurs in dry areas with less than 500mm of annual rain. Open forests with medium-sized trees are found in areas with up to 1,000mm of rain. Tall closed forests including rainforests only appear in regions receiving more than 1,000mm of annual rainfall.

# How are Trees named and grouped?

All tree species known have a botanical and in most cases, but not always, a common name. Common names can be confusing, as trees with a wide distribution range can be known under a number of different names and sometimes the same common name is used for more than one tree species. Furthermore common names can suggest a relation, such as the Red and Yellow Carabeen, which are not closely related, but have a resemblance in the appearance of their timber only. So remembering botanical names is an advantage. Botanical names sort closely related trees into a genus (plural: genera) and related genera into a family, such as *Corymbia* (the genus) *ficifolia* (the species) in the Myrtle family: MYRTACEAE. Species are sometimes further divided into subspecies, variations and forms. Italic fonts are used when printing botanical genus and species names. Tree families are grouped into plant orders and two major subdivisions, i.e. the Gymnosperms, all Conifers, and the Angiosperms, the flowering plants.

# How many Trees and Shrubs exist in Australia?

About 900 Eucalyptus species and nearly 1,000 different Wattle (Acacia) trees are native to Australia. Tropical rainforest tree and shrub species from northern Australia number more than 1,200. Subtropical and other forms of rainforest account for more than 850 different tree species, with an overlap of species occurring in temperate and tropical climates. There are hundreds of species in the protea family (PROTEACEAE), which includes trees and shrubs such as Banksias, Grevilleas and also the Macadamia Nut Tree. Some trees and shrubs have not been described or even been discovered yet. So by any means, trees that call Australia home are numbered in their thousands, making the process of identifying them an interesting challenge.

Springbrook National Park, Queensland.

# What Do I need to Identify Trees?

A digital camera, the one on your mobile phone is probably good enough, to take photographs of important features for later research and comparisons. A notebook to record qualities such as texture, scent of leaves, bark and flowers is helpful. A magnifying glass for closer inspection of samples and a pair of binoculars to observe foliage higher up in a tree may come in handy. Also a ruler and tape measure to note the dimension of leaves, fruits and trunks are useful. Access to a computer

with an internet connection will allow you to compare your plant samples and photographs with listings on tree identification websites. Useful internet resources for more information on tree identification are listed under 'Bibliography and Further Reading'.

Macleay Laurel (*Anopterus macleayanus*) fruit.

# How are Trees and Shrubs identified?

As most of us haven't got access to electron microscopes and DNA sampling equipment the process of identification is based on the physical appearance of plants. The ability to recognise trees in the wild ('in the field') depends on some basic knowledge on how to use plant features in identification. The observation skill needed can be learned and will improve with some practice. Vegetative features used in identification of a native tree or shrub can be divided into a number of categories. They include leaf, flower, fruit, bark characteristics and also the habit (i.e. the size and shape of the tree). Graphical explanations of basic botanical concepts and terminology can be found in the 'Practical Section'.

Leaves and bark play an important role as they are present at any time, and encountering a leafless tree helps in identification, as numbers of Australian deciduous trees are limited. Other means of identification are the preferred habitats, with some species only occurring in close proximity to the coast and others being restricted to higher altitudes or only found in a certain forest type. The geographical distribution is another factor affecting identification, as a number of tree species inhabit a relatively small distribution range. Matching results of different vegetative attributes, preferred habitat and distribution range are the keys to any conclusive plant identification. More detailed information on how to identify tree species is given in the 'Practical Section' at end of this guide.

Top: Tall Nightshade (*Solanum nobile*) flower.          Blackbutt Tree (*Eucalyptus pilularis*) leaves.

# HOW HAVE AUSTRALIAN TREES EVOLVED?

# From the Jurassic Period to the present

It was common belief that Eucalyptus trees (Gum trees) formed the original forests of Australia and that rainforest species had been introduced from Asia. But now it is well accepted that Australia's rainforests rank with the oldest in the world and that they are relics from a primeval time. All trees existing in Australia today are grouped into two major subdivisions, the Gymnosperms, meaning 'naked seed', and the Angiosperms, meaning 'seed in a vessel' in Greek.

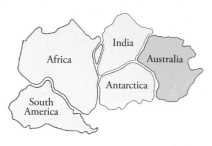

Gondwana
The Great Southern Continent

## Jurassic Period (201 million–145 million years ago)

180 million years ago: Dinosaurs ruled the planet. The supercontinent of Gondwana united South America, Africa, India, Antarctica and Australia. Dating from this time, the oldest Australian tree species still in existence are the Gymnosperms, which do not bear flowers, but develop unprotected egg-cells (ovules) attached to cone scales. This method of reproduction dates back to more than 200 million years ago. The most recognisable trees belonging to this subdivision in Australia are the conifers. They include iconic species such as the Kauri Pine (*Agathis robusta*), Bunya Pine (*Araucaria bidwillii*) in Queensland, Hoop Pine (*Araucaria cunninghamii*) in New South Wales and Queensland and Huon Pine

Wollemi Pine
(*Wollemia nobilis*).

Southern Forest Dragon (*Hypsilurus spinipes*).

(*Lagarostrobos franklinii*) in Tasmania. Clear fossil imprints dating from this time were found at the Talbragar Fish Beds in New South Wales and show surprising similarities with today's conifers. The Wollemi Pine (*Wollemia nobilis*), thought to be extinct, was rediscovered in 1994 and is regarded as a living fossil from this time.

# When did Flowering Plants evolve?

### Cretaceous Period (145 million–66 million years ago)

At the beginning of this period conditions such as worldwide cooling and changing sea-levels started to exert pressure on the continued existence of tall Gymnosperm (conifer) rainforests inhabiting Gondwana.

125 million years ago: The supercontinent of Gondwana had started to break up into the continents we know today. At this time the first flowering plants appeared in what is now central Africa. Australia was still connected to Antarctica and covered in dense Gymnosperm forests with tall cycads and ferns growing beneath.

Treefern Forest at Errinundra, East Gippsland, Victoria.

Antarctic Beech
(*Nothofagus moorei*).

80 million years ago: Australia started to separate from Antarctica, and the rise of the Tasman Sea began to divide New Zealand from the continent. Fossil records from that time indicate that flowering trees, Angiosperms, had evolved and were becoming more widely distributed. In Angiosperms an ovary protects the egg-cells (ovules) and reproductive parts are borne on flowers. Tree families of early Angiosperm origin still make up a large percentage of species found in different forms of Australian rainforests. The Antarctic Beech (*Nothofagus moorei*) is an ancient tree and today is still a dominant species in cool temperate rainforests at higher altitudes. Towards the end of this period the beautiful proteas (Family PROTEACEAE) had evolved. This family of trees includes Banksias, Grevilleas and also the Macadamia Nut Tree. During this time, Australia had a wet warm climate and was covered in primeval rainforest made up of conifers and an increasing number of Angiosperm rainforest trees.

# When did Eucalyptus and Wattle Trees appear?

The Tertiary Period (66 million–2.5 million years ago) is divided into epochs:

### The Paleocene Epoch (66 million–56 million years ago)

At the beginning of the Paleocene epoch the dinosaurs became extinct and the Australian continent started its long and isolated journey north. By now the flowering tree species (Angiosperms) are well in the process of diversifying and displacing conifer forests in Australia. At the end of this epoch the first evidence of eucalypt-like pollen appeared. It is believed that Eucalypts evolved from rainforest trees by adapting to a drier climate. The continent was now totally separated from Antarctica.

Eucalyptus flower

### The Eocene Epoch (56 million–34 million years ago)

Flower, leaf and fruit fossils dating from the Eocene epoch show that the very large family of the Myrtles (MYRTACEAE) was flourishing. Myrtles are currently considered to include all species of Gum trees (*Eucalyptus* sp.), Paperbarks and Tea Trees (*Melaleuca* and *Leptospermum* sp.), but also various rainforest trees. The Australian continent on its way north was changing to a drier climate. The still dominant rainforests started to contract to the East, South and North of the continent and river systems in Western Australia disappeared.

### The Oligocene Epoch (34 million–23 million years ago)

Fossil relics from the Oligocene show evidence that the genus *Acacia* (Family FABACEAE – MIMOSACEAE), commonly known as Wattle trees, evolved in Western Australia. FABACEAE are commonly known as the Pea and Bean family, producing seed pods of all shapes and sizes. Northern parts of Western Australia and inland areas of the continent became more arid and occurrences of wild fires were on the increase.

Black Bean (*Castanospermum australe*) seed pod.

# When did Australia's deserts form?

### The Miocene Epoch (23 million–5 million years ago)

The Australian continent was drying out, making Eucalypt, Acacia and Casuarina trees the dominant species in central Australia. Rainforests were retreating and the continent came into contact with South-East Asia, ending the unique evolution of Australian plants. Plant species from Asia began to migrate to northern parts of the continent.

Arid region in central Australia.

### The Pliocene Epoch (5 million–2.5 million years ago)

After a warmer beginning the climate was cooling globally in the Pliocene Epoch. Cool temperate rainforests were appearing in southern parts of Australia, where the diversity was reduced to just a few dominant tree species. Deserts were forming in the centre of the continent and arid regions were greatly expanding.

### The Pleistocene Epoch (Quaternary period 2.5 million–11,000 years ago)

The Australian continent moved close to the geographical position it is in now. It was the beginning of the latest Ice Age with glacial and warmer interglacial times. Glacial periods are the peaks of cold temperatures worldwide in which the polar caps reach their greatest extent. More than 40,000 years ago the first humans started to inhabit the continent. Only 1 per cent of the Australian landmass was still inhabited by ancient rainforests.

### The Holocene Epoch (11,000 years ago–present)

After the end of the last glacial period, about 10,000 years ago, global temperatures and sea-levels were rising. Tasmania and Papua New Guinea were separated from the Australian mainland again. Aboriginal people would have had a minor effect on vegetation compared to the arrival of Europeans. An estimated 90 per cent of Australian rainforest has disappeared since European settlement began.

Tropical Rainforest.

SUBDIVISION GYMNOSPERMS,
THE CONIFERS

# What are Conifers?

All Australian trees are grouped into two major subdivisions: the Gymnosperms, meaning 'naked seed', and Angiosperms, meaning 'seed in a vessel' in Greek. The oldest Australian tree species in existence today are the Gymnosperms. Australian conifers have an ancient history dating back more than 180 million years. Fossil imprints of twigs and leaves from that time show surprising similarities to trees still in existence today. Conifers are Gymnosperms, which are plants that reproduce by means of male pollen directly fertilising an unprotected ovule (egg-cell). Wind is the primary method by which these trees are pollinated and how their winged seeds are dispersed. With some exceptions they produce woody cones, which are either male or female. The female cone of the Bunya Pine (*Araucaria bidwillii*) can measure more than 30cm long and weigh as much as 3kg. Today old trees are relatively rare because most conifers produce a valuable timber. Only a small percentage of Australian trees are Gymnosperms.

Bunya Pine (*Araucaria bidwillii*) cone.

## Conifers in Family ARAUCARIACEAE

This family includes tall and iconic trees such as the Hoop, Kauri and Bunya Pines. There are only five different species naturally occurring in Australia, which share common ancestors with trees in South America, New Zealand and some South Pacific Islands. Their natural habitat in Australia stretches from the north coast of New South Wales to the Cape York Peninsula in Queensland, although they have been planted in other parts of Australia. They produce woody cones as a fruit and their leaves are stiff in texture, showing faint longitudinal veins. Conifers are relatively slow-growing and can live for a very long time.

# Bunya Pine *Araucaria bidwillii*

This native Australian conifer is well known for its typical dome-shaped crown and large fruit cones which produce edible seeds. The Bunya Pine often forms the highest canopy in its restricted natural habitat of subtropical and tropical rainforests. Competing for available light it is able to reach 45m in height. The bark on the trunk is dark brown and very rough in texture, showing horizontal grooves. The fruit is a large cone measuring up to 35cm long and 20cm in diameter. It is dark green when falling from the tree as a whole fruit, and may not even divide into segments on impact. Individual wedge-shaped segments are referred to

as cone scales and contain a large brown-coloured seed up to 5cm long. Palatable seeds can be eaten raw or roasted. Simple leaves which attach to the stem in a spiral fashion are up to 7cm long, narrow to broadly lance-shaped with entire margins,

dark green, glossy on top, lighter green below, firm and stiff in texture. The leaf apex ends in a sharp spiny tip. Veins run parallel along the length of the leaf blade. This hardy and frost-resistant species has been grown as an ornamental tree along the length of the Australia's east coast and in Tasmania. Distribution: south-eastern and northern Queensland.

## Hoop Pine *Araucaria cunninghamii*

In its natural habitat of different rainforest types this very tall tree can reach a height of up to 60m. It is found from coastal to mountainous locations and often forms the highest level (stratum) in the forest canopy. Naturally it is branchless for up to two-thirds of its height, whereas trees planted in full sunlight hold branches low to the ground. Bark is dark brown or dark grey with a rough texture, and shows horizontal fissures (cracks) forming rings around the trunk. The woody cone consists of layered wedge-shaped cone scales, each containing a brown seed up to 3cm long. Cones take up to 12 months to reach full maturity, but most disintegrate on the branch before falling. Leaves are less than 1cm long, curved dagger-like with entire margins, dark green and stiff in texture. Distribution: New South Wales to north Queensland.

## Kauri Pine (Smooth Bark Kauri, Queensland Kauri) *Agathis robusta*

Within drier forms of subtropical and tropical rainforests this stately tree can attain heights of up to 50m. It is a valuable timber tree, so specimens of this size are rare nowadays. Weathered bark is grey, hard and rather smooth in texture. It is shed in thin flakes exposing the fresh brown-coloured bark. Male cones are made up of numerous tiny scales, turning from green to brown with full maturity. They measure up to 10cm long and reach between 1–1.5cm in diameter. They mature over late winter into spring, often lasting for months beneath the tree, making them a good identification feature. Simple leaves with an opposite arrangement are up to 12cm long, varied in shape from ovate to lance-shaped or elliptical with entire margins, dark green, glossy, thick and leathery in texture. Fine parallel venation is visible on both surfaces. Distribution: north and south-east Queensland.

# Conifers in Family CUPRESSACEAE

## Port Jackson Cypress Pine *Callitris rhomboidea*

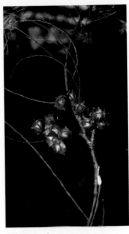

Cypress Pines in the genus *Callitris* are found all over Australia and typically have minute scale-like leaves. The Port Jackson Pine has a wide distribution range and is very adaptable to different environments. It is a shrub or small tree less than 10m high with an attractive and dense canopy. Bark on the trunk of mature trees is brown with older bark weathering to grey. It is rough and firm in texture showing deep longitudinal furrows. The indehiscent (before opening) cone is globe-shaped, glossy, dark greyish-brown and measures about 2cm in diameter. When fully mature it will harden to a woody consistency and split open into six segments (valves). A lens is needed to observe the pointy scale-like leaves arranged in a whorl of three at internodes along branchlets. They only measure 2–3mm long and are dark green. Distribution: Tasmania, Victoria, New South Wales and Queensland.

## Brush Cypress Pine (Stringybark Pine) *Callitris macleayana*

This cypress pine prefers areas with higher rainfall and occurs within and on margins of different rainforest types or in wet tall forests. Under ideal conditions it is a tall tree reaching heights of up to 40m. The distinctive bark has a very rough, furrowed and fibrous texture, especially on the trunk of older trees. It is grey to brown and emits a resinous scent when cut. The female cone measures up to 2.5cm in diameter and hardens to a woody consistency when fully ripe. The cone features a pointed apex and splits open into 6–8 segments (valves). On young trees simple leaves are arranged in a whorl of 3–4 and can be up to 1cm long with a sharply pointed tip. Tiny, scale-like leaves on mature trees only reach 3–5mm long. Distribution: New South Wales and Queensland.

SUBDIVISION ANGIOSPERMS,
THE FLOWERING TREES

EUCALYPTS, PAPERBARKS,
TEA TREES AND BOTTLEBRUSHES,
FAMILY MYRTACEAE

# What are Angiosperms?

All Australian trees are grouped into two major subdivisions: the Angiosperms, meaning 'seed in a vessel' in Greek, and the Gymnosperms, meaning 'naked seed'. In Angiosperms an ovary protects the egg-cells (ovules) and reproductive parts are borne on flowers. The vast majority of Australian trees are Angiosperms.

Eucalyptus leaves

# What are Myrtles, Family MYRTACEAE?

The Myrtles are the largest and most diverse family of Australian trees and include all species of Eucalypt 'Gum trees', Paperbarks, Callistemon 'Bottlebrushes' and Tea Trees. All species have simple leaves, which are normally rather thick and leathery in texture, and often emit a scent when being crushed.

## The Eucalypts, Genus *Eucalyptus* Family MYRTACEAE

# What are Eucalyptus Trees?

Throughout the world Eucalypt forests of all kinds are strongly associated with the Australian landscape. There are more than 900 different Eucalypt species, from moisture-loving forest giants to stunted Mallee woodlands and alpine shrubs. Eucalyptus species have adapted to nearly all climatic conditions and soil types present in Australia. The exceptions are the most arid inland regions and small areas inhabited by different rainforests types. The vast majority of Eucalyptus species only exist in Australia (they are endemic).

# What are Eucalyptus Trees used for?

The essential oil distilled from the leaves is used in the production of perfumes and for medicinal purposes. Many Eucalyptus species yield a durable hardwood timber which is widely used for carpentry, cabinet making and in the building industry. Bees produce beautiful honey from the pollen of the abundant and often sweet scented flowers. Eucalypts are the home and the major food source for Koalas.

Tallowwood (*Eucayptus microcorys*) flower buds.

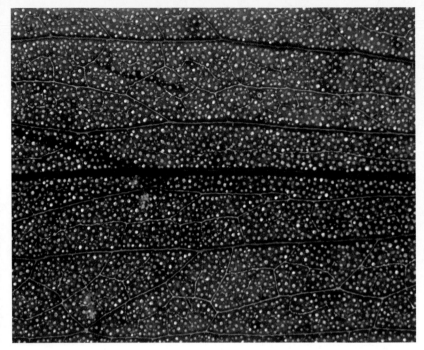

Oil glands of a Eucalyptus leaf.

# What have Eucalyptus Trees in common?

A characteristic of all Eucalypts is the progression (sequence) of different leaf phases, which are referred to as seedling, juvenile, intermediate and adult leaves. There are large differences in the size and shape of these leaves, and a transformation from an opposite to an alternate leaf arrangement occurs. Adult leaves are typically rather thick, smooth and leathery in texture with entire (smooth) margins and an alternate arrangement. Oil glands in leaves are common and can be observed as translucent dots when the leaf is held against the light. These oil glands are responsible for the sticky texture and aromatic scent of many species. While the fruit greatly varies in size and shape, it becomes leathery or woody when mature and releases seeds by opening valves. Many Eucalyptus trees can survive intense fires and after losing all their leaves regenerate from growth buds hidden beneath their bark or can reshoot from root stock (lignotubers).

Eucalyptus leaves, flowers, buds and bark.

# How to identify Eucalyptus Trees?

In general it is relatively easy to recognise a Eucalyptus tree, but to differentiate between species is more difficult. It is done by matching a combination of characteristics such as size and shape (habit), leaves, bark, flower buds and fruit. If no leaves are in reach look around the base of the tree in question for fallen fruit capsules, buds and leaves, but be aware of overlapping tree canopies. Inspect what type of bark is present; take photographs but also remember to take note of scent and texture. Your location might be an important factor as many Eucalypts only have a limited distribution range.

## Messmate (Messmate Stringybark) *Eucalyptus obliqua*

This Eucalypt was the first to be described by a French botanist (Charles-Louis L'Heritier) in 1788. It is one of the tallest of all Eucalyptus species and under ideal conditions can grow to more than 80m high. It can be reduced to the size of a shrub in exposed coastal locations or more commonly is a tree under 50m in tall open forests. The Messmate has a wide distribution range and prefers mountainous locations where it is able to withstand frosts and snow. On a tall tree the trunk (bole) is column-shaped and branchless to half or more of its height. The bark is a reddish-brown with older surfaces weathering to grey. It is rough furrowed, rather soft and fibrous in texture. Up to 15 flower buds are held on a common stalk (peduncle) up to 15mm long. The woody fruit varies from barrel- to urn-shaped and measures up to 12mm long. It has a rough surface and 3–4 slightly sunken valves. Simple adult leaves with an alternate arrangement are up to 15cm long, broadly lance-shaped or curved (falcate), scented when crushed, dark green, semi-glossy on top, a very similar green beneath (concolorous), firm and leathery in texture. The base shape of the leaf is asymmetric (oblique) and the leaf stalk measures up to 20mm long. Distribution: Tasmania, South Australia, Victoria, New South Wales and southern Queensland.

# Snow Gum (Cabbage Gum, White Sally) *Eucalyptus pauciflora*

As the common name implies this shrub or small to medium-sized tree is able to grow at altitudes of 2,000m. Snow Gums prefer mountainous terrain, but in a few locations their natural habitat can extend close to sea-level. Trees growing on exposed sites often form pure stands, creating low woodlands with a canopy height of less than 10m. Here common features are short, crooked trunks with low sturdy branches (limbs) shaped by the prevailing winds. Newly exposed bark is rather smooth and colourful, ranging from white to dark grey with pink and yellow hues. Bark detaches in irregular patches or in short, broad strips. Up to 12 individual flower buds are held on a common stalk (peduncle) reaching 15mm long, whereas individual flower stalks (pedicels) are not present or only very short. The woody fruit is cup-shaped (cupular) or more upside-down cone-shaped (obconical) and measures up to 15mm long. At the top of the fruit, three rounded valves sit level with the rim. They open to release fine, brown, roughly pyramid-shaped seeds. Simple adult leaves show conspicuous longitudinal veins. They are up to 16cm long, lance-shaped, straight or slightly curved, glossy, dark green on both surfaces, strong and leathery in texture. Four subspecies are recognised which mainly differ in the shape of flower buds, fruits and size of leaves. Distribution: Tasmania, South Australia, Victoria, New South Wales and south-eastern Queensland. (Subspecies *pauciflora*, shown, ssp. *niphophila*, ssp. *lacrimans* and ssp. *debeuzevillei*).

## River Red Gum (Murray Red Gum) *Eucalyptus camaldulensis*

Out of all Eucalyptus species the iconic River Red Gum has the widest natural distribution range in mainland Australia. It is common along many inland river systems, except for the east-coast where it is replaced by its close relative the Forest Red Gum (*E. tereticornis*). Massive River Red Gums growing on banks of permanent streams are able to reach 45m, but heights around 20m are more usual. Bark overall is smooth in texture but some rough, dark grey bark can be present on the lower trunk. The distinctive bark colours range from white to grey with patches of browns and reds. A slender common stalk (peduncle) up to 2.5cm long supports groups of 7–12 separate flowers. The woody fruit shows mostly four claw-like valves protruding well past the rim level. Adult leaves are up to 25cm long, lance-shaped and often greyish-green. Distribution: all states except for Tasmania.

## Forest Red Gum (Blue Gum, Queensland) *Eucalyptus tereticornis*

This tall Eucalyptus is widely distributed along Australia's east coast. It grows in coastal regions to mountainous locations and is able to reach a height of 50m. Newly exposed bark is very smooth and has a glossy surface, whereas older bark becomes finely rough and granular in texture. It is different shades of grey and sheds in irregularly sized patches. A short stocking of rough bark is often present at the base of the trunk. Up to ten separate flowers are held on a common stalk measuring up to 3cm long. Flower buds are distinctively cone-shaped and up to 10mm long. The rounded fruit features 4–5 stout and strongly raised valves. Adult leaves with an alternate arrangement are up to 20cm long, lance-shaped, straight or curved (falcate), dull green on top, paler beneath and scented when crushed. Distribution: Victoria to north Queensland.

## Scribbly Gum *Eucalyptus signata*

The characteristic scribbles on the bark of this medium-sized tree are responsible for the common name. They are caused by boring insect larvae and also appear on a number of other Eucalyptus species sharing the same common name. Different species of Scribbly Gums are best recognised by their different shaped and sized flower buds. The natural habitat of the Scribbly Gum (E.signata) includes wetter coastal areas and open forests where it can attain a height of up to 25m. Bark showing the familiar scribbles is white to light grey, smooth and firm in texture. The woody fruit is reverse cone-shaped, small at 5–7mm in diameter and features four valves at about rim level. Adult leaves with an alternate arrangement are up to 15cm long, lance-shaped, scented when crushed, semi-glossy, mid-green on both surfaces, firm and leathery in texture. Distribution: New South Wales and Queensland.

## Blackbutt *Eucalyptus pilularis*

Blackbutt trees are regular in tall open forests and are a vital source of quality hardwood timber for New South Wales. Mature specimens growing on favourable sites are able to reach more than 70m. Fibrous and rough bark covering the base of the trunk is often blackened by bush fires, whereas the normal colour is greyish-brown. The white bark on the top half of the tree is smooth in texture and sheds in long narrow strips, which often still dangle from the upper branches. A common stalk carries up to 15 cigar-shaped flower buds with a shiny and smooth surface. The woody fruit is either egg or cup-shaped and measures around 1cm across, displaying four valves set below rim level. Adult leaves have an alternate arrangement and are up to 18cm long, lance-shaped, straight or curved, and scented when crushed. Distribution: New South Wales and Queensland.

## Blue Gum (Sydney Blue Gum) *Eucalyptus saligna*

On first impression the very tall Blue Gum is rather similar in appearance to the Flooded Gum (*E. grandis*). Often both species share a habitat of moist tall forests and transition zones around rainforests. Distinguishing features of the Blue Gum are the bluish-grey flecks and streaks in the bark, which become more pronounced in wet weather. A short, rough-barked stocking at the base is firm, smooth and dark grey. The small, woody fruit is only 5mm wide, less than 1cm long and shows variation in form from champagne glass- to barrel-shaped. After opening, 3–4 thin valve tips protrude above the rim level. Simple adult leaves are up to 18cm long with entire margins, narrow elliptic in shape, straight or slightly curved, mid-green above, paler beneath, scented when crushed and rather stiff in texture. Distribution: southern New South Wales to Queensland.

## Flooded Gum (Rose Gum) *Eucalyptus grandis*

Favouring moist and fertile soils, the Flooded Gum is often the first Eucalyptus species found around rainforest margins. It is a very tall tree attaining heights of 70m with a straight trunk devoid of major branches for more than half of its height. Bark is a relatively uniform whitish-grey with a very smooth and hard texture. In periods of prolonged rain, bark colour changes to a darker grey with an olive-green hue. A stocking of rough, fibrous bark is normally retained at the base of the tree. The woody fruit measures only about 5mm in diameter and is upside-down cone-shaped. After opening, five stout pointed and incurved valve tips are slightly exerted above the rim level. Adult leaves with an alternate arrangement are up to 16cm long, lance-shaped with entire margins, mid-green, dull above, paler green beneath, scented, strong and rigid in texture. Distribution: southern New South Wales to north Queensland.

## Mountain Ash (Stringy Gum) *Eucalyptus regnans*

After the Redwoods of California this Australian Eucalypt is the tallest tree on the planet, able to reach 100m in height. Dense stands of this species, together with an understorey of smaller trees and ferns can create a tall closed forest. The Mountain Ash is a valuable timber tree producing a quality hardwood, which is used for a range of building purposes. The base of the trunk is covered by rough and stringy bark extending up to 15m in height. Higher up the whitish bark is smooth in texture and sheds in long narrow strips. Up to 15 flower buds are supported by a single stalk up to 13mm long. The woody fruit is typically half rounded in shape and less than 1cm across. Adult leaves are up to 15cm long, broadly lance-shaped, straight or sometimes curved (falcate) and the same glossy green on both surfaces. Distribution: Tasmania and Victoria.

## Karri *Eucalyptus diversicolor*

The natural habitat of the Karri is restricted to high rainfall areas around the southern tip of Western Australia. It is the tallest tree in that state and plays an important role in the commercial production of hardwood timber. Exceptional trees have been

recorded at more than 80m tall, but heights of around 60m are more usual. Compared to other Eucalypts the Karri is vulnerable to intensive fires, as it is not able to regenerate from buds hidden under the bark or from underground rootstock (lignotubers). The ornamental bark is smooth all over the tree and multi-coloured; ranging from white to grey with reddish, yellow and orange patches. The woody fruit is barrel-shaped and measures up to 12mm long. Typically three valves are set below rim level. Adult leaves are up to 12cm long, broadly lance-shaped, dark green above and paler green below. Distribution: Western Australia.

## The Bloodwoods, Genus *Corymbia*

# What are Bloodwood Trees?

Trees belonging to this genus produce the urn-shaped fruits generally known and often depicted as 'Gum nuts'. Combined with the thin paper-fruited and woody-fruited species about 90 different trees belong to this genus. Bloodwoods have a wide distribution range and exist in every state except Tasmania. Their habitat ranges from arid regions in central Australia to high rainfall areas along the east-coast and in the tropical north. Most range in size from small to medium trees, but some are able to reach a height of 40m or more.

## Red-flowering Gum (Scarlet-flowering Gum)
### *Corymbia ficifolia*

The stunning flowers and its compact size have made this tree a popular ornamental plant in many parts of Australia. Naturally it only occurs in a relatively small area in the south-west of Western Australia, but has proven to be very adaptable to different climates and soil types. In cultivation it rarely reaches more than 10m high, forming a densely foliated and multi-branching crown. Bark on mature trees is brown and has a rough, stringy texture. Flowers are dominated by a ring of numerous pink-, orange- or scarlet-coloured stamens. Open flowers can reach more than 5cm in diameter and bloom over summer and autumn. The large urn-shaped fruit measures more than 4cm long, up to 3cm in diameter and contains dark brown seeds surrounded by a papery wing. Adult leaves are broadly lance-shaped and up to 14cm long. Distribution: Western Australia.

# Ghost Gum (Aparrerinja, White gum) *Corymbia aparrerinja*

The striking appearance and the vast but sparse distribution make the Ghost Gum a stand-out feature in the central Australian landscape. It can be a medium-sized tree surrounded by low, scrubby vegetation or a small tree growing on rocky ground. The botanical name *aparrerinja* is a derivation of the Aboriginal word for the Ghost Gum, which plays an important part in their culture. The trunk and branches are covered in smooth, white bark with small light brown to grey patches. White flowers are held on multi-branching stalks emerging from leaf axils towards the end of branches. Flowering period is over summer. The thin-walled fruit which takes about 12 months to mature is urn- or barrel-shaped and measures up to 15mm long. Adult leaves are up to 16cm long, narrowly lance-shaped and the same glossy green on both surfaces. Distribution: central Northern Territory, Queensland and Western Australia.

## Pink Bloodwood *Corymbia intermedia*

The Pink Bloodwood is a medium-sized tree with a far-reaching distribution range along Australia's east coast. It is able to reach up to 35m in height and is found in tall open forests from the coastline to the higher ranges. A rough and distinct scaly bark is a pale greyish to light brown. Small patches of resin (kino) can be present. Sweet fragrant flowers are held in groups of up to seven on a common stalk. The woody fruit is mostly urn-shaped and measures up to 2cm long. The outer surface is very rough, being covered in small warts and whitish speckles. Seeds are reddish-brown and enclosed in a translucent, papery wing. Adult leaves are up to 16cm long, lance-shaped, mostly straight, dark green on top, paler beneath, leathery and faintly scented. This tree is similar in appearance to the Red Bloodwood (*C. gummifera*). Distribution: New South Wales to north Queensland.

## The Paperbarks Genus *Melaleuca*

# What are Melaleucas?

Melaleucas are found all over Australia with habitats ranging from dry inland regions to wet coastal areas. In general, species growing in dry conditions, especially in Western Australia, are only shrubs or small trees, whereas medium and tall species prefer wetter environments. Some tree species are found in tidal swamps and are tolerant to salt spray from the ocean. Melaleucas are well-known for their essential oils, in particular *Melaleuca alternifolia*, the familiar Tea Tree. The common name Tea Tree can be confusing as it is also used for trees in the genus *Leptospermum*.

Paperbark swamp forest.

# How to identify Paperbark Trees?

Most but not all of the 250 species existing here have the typically thin and very paper-like bark. Flowers are characteristically dominated by bundles of stamens which are predominantly white or cream-coloured, and less frequently in a range of other hues. Groups of individual flowers form a cylindrical spike or a rounded head at the end of branches, which continue growing. The fruit is a capsule which splits open to reveal multiple valves (segments) at the top, each containing a large number of fine seeds.

It becomes woody with maturity and is usually rounded or more egg-shaped. Clusters of old capsules can remain on branches for a long time, making them a useful identification feature. The leaves of most species are alternate and have entire (smooth) margins. However, size and shape varies greatly from short, thin and needle-like to broad and elongated.

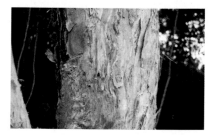

Five-veined Paperbark (*Melaleuca quinquenervia*).

## Long-leaved Paperbark *Melaleuca leucadendra*

As one of the tallest species in the *Melaleuca* genus, this tree is able to reach more than 40m in height. Its natural habitat includes tropical lowland Paperbark forest, swamps and areas along tidal waterways. Here this species is a tall tree, whereas in drier and less fertile environments it may be less than 20m high. Bark is whitish-grey and typically soft and papery in texture. Pure white flowers change to a cream colour with age and emerge on spikes measuring up to 15cm long. Spaced out groups of capsules mature to a woody consistency and turn brown. They are cylindrical or short barrel-shaped and measure less than 0.5cm long. Simple leaves with an alternate arrangement are up to 20cm long, narrowly lance-shaped, straight or only slightly curved, dull, mid-green with a grey hue, thick and leathery in texture. Distribution: tropical Queensland, Northern Territory and Western Australia.

## Prickly-leaved Myrtle *Melaleuca nodosa* (Ball Honey-myrtle, Yellow Myrtle)

This species is a multi-stemmed shrub which rarely grows to more than 4m high and prefers drier habitats. It is commonly found in heath lands close to the coast and further inland in dry open Eucalypt-dominated forests. The compact size, low water requirements and beautiful flowers make this species an interesting garden plant. Bark on older stems shows areas of a very thick paper-like texture but otherwise stems and branches are rather smooth and soft. Appearing at the end of young branches are attractive rounded flower-heads which are cream to more yellow-coloured and blossom over spring into summer. Tight groups of small and persistent woody fruits (capsules) are held along branches, creating a rounded shape. The alternately arranged and stiff leaves feature a spiny tip at the apex. They are up to 4cm long, oblong in shape, straight and scented when crushed. Distribution: South Australia, New South Wales and Queensland.

# Five-veined Paperbark *Melaleuca quinquenervia*

Also known as the Broad-leaved Paperbark, this adaptive tree is common in wetter coastal areas such as swamps, marshes and tidal waterways, where it will often form pure stands. Under ideal conditions it can attain a height of 25m, but if growing in drier locations such as headlands, it may only reach half that size. In exposed coastal positions the trunk and limbs often bend the way of the prevailing winds. Thin papery bark covers the whole tree with the outer layers being whitish to pale grey, whereas the newly exposed bark is salmon-coloured. Spectacular flowers display a bundle of pure white stamens which appear along the same branch holding last season's fruit. Main flowering period is over the winter months. The dark brown woody fruit reaches up 5mm in diameter. It is a half-rounded capsule showing slightly exerted valve tips at the apex. Old capsules, after releasing their seed, can remain on branches for years. Leaves with an alternate arrangement are up to 9cm long, broad elliptic to more reverse lance-shaped (oblanceolate), mostly straight or rarely curved, thick, leathery in texture and emit a strong scent when crushed. Five longitudinal veins are more noticeable on the lower leaf surface. This species is used for beach and headland re-vegetation. Distribution: New South Wales central coast to north Queensland.

# Tea Tree *Melaleuca alternifolia* (Narrow-leaved Paperbark)

This shrub or small tree produces the valuable medicinal Tea Tree oil, which is well-known and used in many parts of the world. On plantations Tea Trees are mechanically harvested before the oil is distilled from the leaves. However, Tea Trees are still manually harvested, as has been the case for nearly a century. Naturally this tree occurs in wet locations such as banks of coastal waterways and marshlands. Here it often forms dense stands and competing for light may reach 15m in height. Yet growing on dry rocky ground it is often only a multi-stemmed shrub. The bark is characteristic for the *Melaleuca* genus, peeling off in thin layered sheets and being white to light grey. Short spikes appearing towards the end of young branches hold up to 30 individual pure white flowers, which blossom from late winter into spring. The woody fruit (a capsule) is rounded and only measures 3–4mm in diameter. Simple leaves are alternate and form rough whorls along branches. They are up to 3cm long, narrow linear with entire margins, dark green, hairless when mature, scented when crushed, thin and soft in texture. Numerous whitish, translucent oil glands can be seen when holding the leaf against the light. Distribution: north-eastern New South Wales.

## The Bottlebrushes Genus *Callistemon*

# How to recognise a Bottlebrush?

The genera *Callistemon* and *Melaleuca*
are closely related and it can be difficult
to distinguish between the two.
However, there are a few characteristics
which help in identification such as
the difference in bark texture. The
bark of Bottlebrushes is rough and
stringy compared to the often papery
texture of Melaleucas. Stamens, the
male reproductive part of a flower, are
frequently longer, creating cylindrical

flower-spikes which are larger in diameter. Colours are more likely to be reds and
bright yellows than white. The leaves of Callistemon have lateral (cross) veins
instead of the frequent longitudinal venation of Melaleucas. Many of the 40 different
Callistemon species existing in Australia make a beautiful addition to any garden.

## Crimson Bottlebrush *Callistemon citrinus*

This handsome shrub is common near the coastline and prefers moist locations in
low-lying areas. The mid-brown bark on the lower trunk is rough. The charming
flower-spikes have the distinctive bottlebrush-like appearance and measure up to
15cm long. Individual flowers are made up of numerous crimson-coloured stamens,
with the long flowering period lasting from spring into autumn. The cup-shaped
fruit measures up to 6mm in diameter and turns woody when fully mature. Valves
at the top of the capsule open to release a large amount of very fine, brown seed.
Old capsules will not fall, but remain on branches for years. Simple leaves with

an alternate arrangement are up to
8cm long, reverse lance-shaped, the
same colour green on both surfaces
(concolorous), strongly scented and
rigid in texture. Midrib is yellowish
on the underside and lateral veins are
present, oil glands are clearly visible.
Distribution: Victoria, New South Wales
and Queensland.

## The Tea Trees Genus *Leptospermum*

# How are Tea Trees identified?

In Australia most of the 80 species belonging to this genus are found in the southern parts of the continent. With a few exceptions most species are actually only shrubs despite their common name. Their vast habitat stretches from sand dunes to altitudes of more than 1,500m with regular frost and snowfalls. The characteristic white or pink flowers feature five rounded petals in contrast to the brush-shaped flower-spikes of Melaleuca and Callistemon species. The firm to woody capsule is supported by a short stalk and doesn't form large clusters. Leaves are regularly small in size, scented and have an alternate arrangement. Confusingly the Tea Tree yielding the popular antibacterial oil is a *Melaleuca* species. (Different spellings of the name Tea Tree are in use).

## Coast Tea Tree *Leptospermum laevigatum*

Being able to tolerate strong salt spray, the Coast Tea Tree is frequently part of the first shrubby vegetation beyond the beach. Older multi-stemmed shrubs often display a spreading habit and can form dense vegetation along sand dunes. The rough and stringy bark sheds in long strips and is cream to a grey-brown. Flowers, measuring up to 20mm in diameter, feature five pure white and rounded petals. The fruit, a stalked capsule is less than 1cm in diameter and will not remain on the

branch for long. Simple leaves are up to 25mm long, mostly reverse lance-shaped, dull grey-green and firm in texture. Distribution: Tasmania, South Australia, Victoria, New South Wales and Queensland.

## The Angophoras or 'Apples' Genus *Angophora*

# What have Angophoras in common?

On first impression, trees belonging to this genus resemble Eucalypts and indeed Angophoras are closely related to the Bloodwood trees. Nevertheless there are reliable traits which set them apart. Angophoras have a regular opposite leaf arrangement and only a very faint scent is emitted when leaves are crushed. Also on closer inspection flowers feature five small petals and the ribbed fruit is more likely to be thin-walled. Angophoras  are a relatively small group of mostly medium-sized trees which are confined to the eastern half of Australia.

## Smooth-barked Apple (Sydney Red Gum, Smooth-barked Angophora) *Angophora costata*

Found in a large range of different habitats, the Smooth-barked Apple can attain a height of 25m, but on poor or rocky sites can have a short and twisted trunk. The distinctive bark  is orange to pink after shedding in large patches, then turning grey with age. Newly exposed areas have a hard and smooth texture (most other Angophoras have rough bark). Individual flowers are borne on multi-branching stalks (panicles) developing at the very end of branches. The hard fruit is on average 15mm long, about 12mm in diameter and features five pronounced ridges, extending past the rim level. Oppositely arranged adult leaves are up to 10cm long, lance-shaped (sometimes curved) with entire margins, dark green and semi glossy on top, paler below with a firm and leathery texture. Mid-vein shows prominently on both leaf surfaces with numerous straight lateral veins only faintly visible. Distribution: (two subspecies) New South Wales and Queensland.

## Turpentine Trees Genus *Syncarpia*

# What are Turpentine Trees?

Turpentine trees are frequently part of moist Eucalypt-dominated forests, where they have the potential to grow very tall. They are substantially reduced in size if growing in drier, more arid environments. Turpentine trees are well-adapted to even intense fires as they are protected by a thick bark which does not easily ignite. The name Turpentine is due to the pungent smell of the resinous timber. As a durable wood it is sought-after for marine purposes such as piers and wooden jetties.

Distinguishing features are the unusually shaped fruit and leaves arranged in a whorl.

## Turpentine *Syncarpia glomulifera*

Exceptional trees of this species can attain a height of more than 50m. Bark is reddish to light brown with a very stringy and fibrous texture. Gorgeous rounded white flowers measure up to 25mm across. Mostly four flowers are held on separate stalks at the end of young branches. At most times of year the strangely-shaped and woody fruit can be found around the base of the tree. The fruit is a useful aid in the identification of this species. Simple leaves are arranged in a whorl of four when emerging, changing to an opposite arrangement thereafter. Leaves are up to 10cm long, mainly egg-shaped (ovate) with entire margins, dark green, hairless on top, whitish hairy on their underside, firm, thick and leathery. The mid-vein is strongly raised on the lower leaf surface.

45

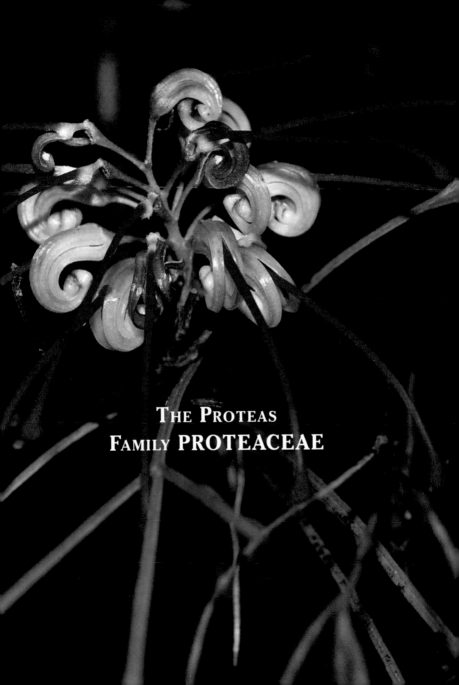

THE PROTEAS
FAMILY **PROTEACEAE**

Waratah flower

# What are Proteas?

This family is one of the largest and most varied in Australia and probably best-known for its strikingly beautiful and unusual flowers. Proteas share common ancestors with plants preferring dry environments in South Africa and moisture-loving rainforest trees in South America. Members of this family include the well-known Grevilleas and Banksias, rainforest species such as Waratahs (*Alloxylon* and *Telopea* sp.), and Macadamia Nuts (*Macadamia* sp.), which are listed in the rainforest section of this guide.

# What are Banksias?

More than 170 species of Banksias only exist in Australia (are endemic), with about 60 species occurring in Western Australia alone. They range in size from small shrubs to medium-sized trees. The genus was named in honour of Sir Joseph Banks, the botanist accompanying Captain Cook on his first expedition in 1770. Banksias and their cultivars are widely used in landscaping for their attractive flower-heads. The abundant nectar produced will attract birds such as Honeyeaters and Lorikeets to the garden.

# How are Banksias indentified?

Coast Banksia (*Banksia integrifolia*) flower.

Flowers are produced at most times of year, with hundreds packed tightly together into each cylindrical spike. Typical colours are yellow, orange and red. Fertilised flowers develop into a woody fruit, a follicle splitting on one side to release flattened and winged seeds. These follicles are stacked horizontally to form a cone-like structure which remains after the seed has dispersed. Leaves, especially on young plants, are often toothed and mostly thick and rather stiff in texture.

## Coast Banksia *Banksia integrifolia*

The Coast Banksia can attain a height of 15m in more sheltered positions, whereas in exposed coastal conditions it only develops into a windblown and twisted shrub less than 5m tall. Bark on older specimens is a light grey, deeply fissured and firm. Cylindrical flower-spikes measure up to 10cm long and are a pale to rather bright yellow. A number of woody fruits (follicles) are stacked in a cone-like group, each releasing two winged seeds. Simple leaves form a whorl of up to six below the growing bud, turning to an alternate arrangement thereafter. Leaves are up to 18cm long, reverse lance-shaped with entire (toothed in juveniles) margins, dark green, hairless on top, light grey and finely hairy below, firm and leathery in texture. Distribution: widespread in coastal Tasmania, Victoria, New South Wales and Queensland.

## Swamp Banksia *Banksia robur*

This attractive green Banksia is a native shrub under 3m tall and prefers wet, swampy locations in coastal areas. Bark is grey with a firm and rather rough texture featuring small fissures (cracks). Beautiful large flower-spikes are cylindrical and up to 20cm long. They are golden-yellow and most plentiful over autumn and winter. Simple leaves develop in a whorl beneath the growing bud and turn to an alternate arrangement thereafter. Leaves are large at 35cm or more long, elliptic with irregular toothed margins, dark green, hairless, fairly glossy on top, pale yellow to cream and velvety hairy beneath, very firm and stiff in texture. The yellow mid-rib and lateral veins are covered in short fine hair. Leaf teeth end in strong, sharp callous spines. Distribution: New South Wales and Queensland.

## The Grevilleas Genus *Grevillea*

# What are Grevilleas?

Silky Oak (*Grevillea robusta*) timber grain.

Nearly all of the 350 native Grevillea species exist only in Australia (endemic). Most of them are only shrub-sized and occur in a range of different climates, from dry and often rocky environments to lush rainforests. The tallest tree in this genus is the familiar Silky Oak (*Grevillea robusta*), which is able to reach heights of 40m. It is a popular street tree producing masses of golden-yellow flowers in spring. The Silky Oak yields a valuable timber known for its intricate wood grain. Native Grevilleas and their many cultivars are excellent garden shrubs with showy and amazing flowers in an incredible range of different colours. For this reason they have been cultivated in many other countries. A number of Grevillea species have a very restricted distributions and some are endangered.

# How are Grevilleas distinguished?

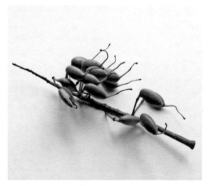

Grevillea fruit.

Groups of flowers are held on a raceme, a spike with each flower borne on an individual stalk. Together they either have a somewhat spidery, insect-like appearance or form a more brush-like shape. The fruit (a follicle) is hairy and often brightly coloured at first, but ripens to a woody consistency and changes to brown. It is supported by a stalk and nearly always topped by a remaining hardened flower style. Typically, follicles contain flattened and often winged seeds. Leaves come in all shapes and sizes, from large and deeply lobed (dissected) to small, stiff and prickly, making them more useful in the recognition of individual species.

# Byfield Spider Flower *Grevillea venusta*

This large shrub or small multi-trunked tree is one of the best examples in showing how astonishing and remarkable flowers of Grevillea species can be. Bark is beige-brown, rough with fissures, blisters and cracks showing a reddish-brown under-layer. Spidery, green and bright yellow flowers with long blue styles are covered in white hair and held together on a raceme up to 10cm long. In the beginning the vividly coloured fruit is covered in long fine hair, but matures as a hard brownish follicle up to 15mm long. Simple leaves with an alternate arrangement are more than 20cm long, narrow lance-shaped with either entire or deeply lobed margins, medium thick and fairly firm, dark green, glossy on top, pale green beneath and mostly hairless. Venation overall is faint. Distribution: only occurs naturally in a small area in central Queensland.

# Fern Leaf Grevillea *Grevillea longifolia*

The very distinctive foliage with long and deeply serrated leaves gives this shrub its characteristic appearance. It is popular as a relative hardy and very ornamental garden shrub, although naturally it is rare and has a limited distribution. Bark is reddish-brown with a rough fibrous and fissured texture. Stunning deep pink to red flowers are borne on toothbrush-like racemes up to 8cm long. Main flowering period is from late winter to early summer. The fruit (a follicle) turns blotchy brown when fully mature and reaches 12mm long. Simple leaves with an alternate arrangement are more than 20cm long, very narrowly elliptic to oblong with irregular toothed margins, deep green, glossy and firm to stiff in texture. Lower leaf surface is silvery-white and features a prominently raised mid-vein. Distribution: central coast of New South Wales. A Threatened Species.

## White Oak *Grevillea baileyana*

Originating from tropical Queensland this small to medium-sized tree is widely used as an ornamental species along Australia's east coast. Noted for their beautiful foliage and flower display, trees grow up to 30m tall in their natural habitat competing for light. Whereas for trees planted in open locations a height of less than 15m is normal.

Bark on the lower trunk of older specimens is hard, scaly and fissured in texture. Bark on branches and young trees is smoother and grey. Pleasantly scented flower racemes are cream or pale yellow, up to 15cm long and appear at the end of young branches. Depending on location the flowering period lasts from late winter to early summer. The fruit is a follicle splitting at one side only and measures up to 15mm long. It contains two flattened and winged seeds which are brown when fully mature. The very attractive leaves are deeply lobed (dissected) on young trees and sometimes are also present on older specimens. Simple adult leaves with an alternate arrangement are between 10–20cm long (juvenile up to 30cm), lance-shaped with entire margins, mid- to dark green, hairless on top, bronze to rust-brown and hairy beneath with a strong firm texture. Leaf apex tapers into a fine point. Mid-vein is hairy and raised on lower leaf surface. Distribution: tropical northern Queensland.

## Red Spider Flower (Olive Grevillea) *Grevillea oleoides*

The Red Spider Flower or Olive Grevillea is an eye-catching native shrub with foliage that has a resemblance to Olive trees. It can reach up to 3m high and has a small distribution range, preferring moist locations within open Eucalypt dominated forests. Bark is grey to light brown with fine fissures (cracks) and a rough texture. Splendid dark pink or red flowers feature a long prominent style and blossom over winter to early spring. Groups of up to 10 individual flowers are supported by a common stalk measuring up to 4cm long. Leaves with an alternate arrangement are up to 12cm long, mostly linear with entire incurved margins, mid-green, dull on top, grey-green, finely hairy beneath and firm in texture. Mid-vein is strongly raised on lower leaf surface, otherwise venation is very faint. Distribution: southern areas of Sydney south to Robertson, New South Wales.

## Red Silky Oak (Banks Grevillea) *Grevillea banksii*

The interesting fern-like appearance of the foliage combined with the spectacular flowers has made this species a well-known ornamental plant. This shrub originates

from the tropical north and grows to a height of 4m. It has been used in the creation of cultivated garden plants, such as the popular and hardy Grevillea 'Honey Gem'. Cuttings are taken to keep plants true to form, as propagation from seed can be variable. Bark is brown, hard with vertical fissures (cracks) and rough in texture. Vibrant pinkish-red to deep red flowers are arranged in a brush-like shape (a raceme) of up to 20cm long. The woody fruit (a follicle) reaches up to 2cm long and is topped by the typical remaining flower style. Deeply divided leaves are more than 20cm long, dark green on top and whitish beneath. Distribution: north Queensland

THE WATTLES (ACACIA)
FAMILY MIMOSACEAE

# What are Wattle (Acacia) Trees?

Acacia trees have adapted to the harshest and driest regions all over Australia and have the ability to regenerate after fires. There are up to 1,000 different Wattle trees (Acacia sp.) native to Australia and the majority of them only exist here (they are endemic). Wattle trees are relatively short-lived, on average only 25–50 years, but some species can live more than 100 years. Most Acacias only reach the height of tall shrubs to medium-sized trees and relatively few occur in rainforests. Arid shrublands dominated by small Wattle trees are known as a Mulga or as a Myall (scrub) in Western Australia. A substantial number of Acacia species don't have a common name or share the same.

Wattle (Acacia) phyllode gland.

## What have Wattle Trees in common?

All Acacia species are legumes, a trait shared with members of the pea and bean family (FABACEAE). Legumes have the ability to extract nitrogen from the air and make it available in the soil by means of root nodules containing nitrogen-fixing bacteria. Trees and shrubs will produce pods of different shapes and sizes, which split at two sides to release their seed. All Acacia trees have a bi-pinnate (fern-like) leaf as an emerging seedling, which is retained by some species into adulthood. The seed needs to be heated by a fire in the wild, or in cultivation scalded with boiling water to germinate. Wattle seeds can stay dormant for more than 20 years awaiting the right conditions to sprout.

Acacia pod.

# How are Acacia Trees identified?

Acacia flower spikes

Acacia flower heads

The botanical term for a Wattle leaf is a phyllode, which is classified as a flattened and expanded leaf stalk. The bi-pinnate, fern-like foliage retained on mature plants is a good identification feature for some species, but most Acacias will develop simple leaves (phyllodes) with age. Leaves vary from small, thin and needle-like to large and broadly ovate (egg-shaped) in form. Smooth edges and an alternate leaf arrangement are also typical for the genus. A small gland (swelling) which is often present at the base of the leaf and the pattern of nerves (veins) are useful features in classification. If present, trees can be recognised by their flowers, which are either held on a cylindrical spike or in rounded flower-heads. Pods play an important role in identification as they can last a considerable time on the ground or can still be found hanging on branches.

# What are Wattle Trees used for?

Acacia species are commonly planted for their striking and abundant flowers, which are mostly cream to bright golden-yellow. They are also frequently used as roadside vegetation for their manageable size, hardiness and low water requirements. On farms in the outback, the leaves of some Wattle trees are eaten by livestock such as sheep and cattle. The hard inner wood was and still is being used by indigenous Australians to fabricate boomerangs, spears and other tools. Some taller Acacia species yield a valuable timber, which is used in cabinet-making.

# Blackwood (Sally Wattle, Mudgerabah) *Acacia melanoxylon*

Due to its wide distribution range this Acacia tree is known under an array of common names. Blackwood grows in various habitats ranging from dry open shrublands to rainforests. In arid regions it is a woody shrub less than 4m high, but in Tasmania it is able to reach the size of a tall tree. Bark on mature trees is grey to brown, hard and furrowed (grooved) at the base. Rounded flower-heads are cream to pale yellow and can consist of more than 50 individual flowers. Groups of up to five flower-heads are held on a common

stalk (a raceme). Flowering period is over spring in cooler climates and over winter in warmer areas. Fruit pods can be found on the forest floor at most times of the year and are helpful when identifying this species. Pods can be twisted or shaped into coils and reach up to 12cm long (when twisted), containing a number of shiny black seeds. Seedlings show fern-like (bi-pinnate) foliage at first, but change to a simple leaf (phyllode) thereafter. Leaves on mature trees feature an alternate arrangement. They are up to 15cm long, narrow reverse lance-shaped or elliptic with entire margins, straight or sickle-shaped (falcate), hairless and fairly thin but firm in texture. Venation is longitudinal. Blackwood yields an excellent timber for fine woodwork. Distribution: South Australia, Victoria, Tasmania, New South Wales and Queensland.

## Mulga Wattle *Acacia aneura*

The name Mulga is not only used for this Wattle tree, but also for tall scrublands (Mulga scrub) found in arid regions of Central Australia. It has adapted to the harshest environments and is able to survive on very poor soils with minimal rainfall. Depending on conditions it can be a relatively long-lived multi-stemmed shrub or a small tree. Bark becomes rough at the base of older trees and is grey if not blackened by fire. The yellow flower-spikes are cylindrical and up to 2cm long. Flowering and successive fruiting depends more on rainfall than on season. Pods are broad and flattened, measuring up to 8cm long and about 2cm in width. They produce edible seeds which were a viable food source for Aboriginal people. Leaves (phyllodes) differ greatly in size and shape, making them unsuitable as a reliable identification feature. Distribution: Western Australia, Northern Territory, South Australia, New South Wales and Queensland.

## Green Wattle *Acacia decurrens* (Early Black Wattle, Wattah)

This medium-sized Wattle tree retains its beautiful bi-pinnate (fern-like) foliage throughout its lifespan. It has been planted for its attractive appearance in many parts of Australia, but is now also found in forests far beyond its natural distribution range. Under good conditions it can reach 20m high with a dense and bright green canopy. The distinctive bark on branches of older and also on the trunk of younger trees is smooth and green. It shows hard and brown ridges running lengthwise. More than 20 individual golden-coloured and rounded flower-heads are arranged at the end of multi-branching stalks (racemes or panicles). Flower period is over winter into spring. Pods reaching 10cm long are flattened and straight. The foliage consists of narrow, oblong leaflets up to 1.5cm long. Distribution: central and southern New South Wales. The common name Green Wattle is shared with *Acacia irrorata*.

# Sydney Golden Wattle (Sallow Wattle) *Acacia longifolia*

The beautiful Sydney Golden Wattle is widely used for landscaping purposes and often planted as roadside vegetation. In exposed coastal conditions this species may only reach 3–4m high, but it can develop into a small tree when growing within tall open forests. It has a large, natural distribution range, including coastal plains and the foothills of the Great Dividing Range. Bark is grey to brown with a firm and slightly rough texture. The abundant golden-yellow flowers appearing over late winter into spring make the Sydney Golden Wattle very noticeable. Flower-spikes are cylindrical and up to 5cm long. The thin, straight pods are rounded and up to 15cm long. Alternatively arranged leaves (phyllodes) are up to 20cm long, narrow elliptic with entire margins, straight or slightly curved, strong and leathery in texture. Distribution: Tasmania, South Australia, Victoria, New South Wales and Queensland. There are two subspecies: *A. longifolia and sophorae*.

## Maiden's Wattle *Acacia maidenii*

This Acacia is able to tolerate high rainfall, but is also found within open forests of drier regions. It can reach up to 15m high and in open positions forms a dense rounded crown. Bark is greyish-brown and becomes rather stringy and fissured on older specimens. Attractive flower-spikes are up to 6cm long, changing from white and cream-coloured to a pale yellow with age. Pods are up to 15cm long, cylindrical and show longitudinal grooves on the surface. They turn brittle and may twist with age, before splitting to release dark brown, oblong seeds. Simple alternately arranged leaves (phyllodes) are up to 18cm long, mostly narrow elliptic in shape, straight or sometimes curved and slightly stiff in texture. Venation is rather faint with up to five longitudinal main veins being more obvious. Distribution: Victoria (rare), New South Wales and Queensland.

## Golden Wattle *Acacia pycnantha*

The large golden-coloured flower-heads and the hardiness of this tall shrub have made it a popular ornamental plant. It has naturalised outside of its original distribution range to many other parts of the continent including Western Australia. Being declared the national flora emblem in 1988 has further added to its status. Bark is brown and on older plants becomes rough and fissured at the base. Gorgeous scented flower-heads are rounded and arranged on a common stalk (a raceme) up to 15cm long. Pods are mainly straight and flattened reaching up to 12cm long. They mature over summer and contain a number of oblong and shiny black seeds. Simple leaves (phyllodes) are distinctive for this species showing an off-centre mid-rib and prominent lateral veins. They are up to 18cm long, reverse lance-shaped, straight or slightly curved, thick and leathery in texture. Distribution: South Australia, Victoria, ACT and southern New South Wales.

## Hickory Wattle (Lightwood) *Acacia implexa*

This widespread shrub or small tree is very adaptable to different climates and environments. It is common along rural roads, in open forests and woodlands. Bark

is grey to brown with a hard and rough texture. Attractive white to pale yellow flower-heads are rounded (globose) and measure about 15mm in diameter. Groups of up to six separate flower-heads are held on a common stalk (raceme) with individual stalks up to 3cm long. Pods can be coiled or twisted and reach up to 15cm long. They turn hard and brown before splitting at the sides to release black, oval-shaped seeds. Alternately arranged simple leaves (phyllodes) are up to 18cm long, very narrow, elliptical and show a small gland on one side of the base. Distribution: Victoria, New South Wales and Queensland.

THE CASUARINAS, SHE-OAKS,
FAMILY **CASUARINACEAE**

# What are Casuarinas?

More than 60 species in this family are native to Australia, with the genera *Casuarina* and *Allocasuarina* being the most important ones. She-oaks are frequently found along the coastline and in more arid inland zones. They are mostly small or medium-sized trees, with the exceptions being the River She-oak, which is a tall tree up to 40m in height. Their characteristic foliage is made up of needle-like branchlets with minute scale-like leaves, making Casuarinas similar in appearance to the Cypress Pines. The wood resembles that of the European Oak, hence the name She-oak. The timber is useful for cabinet-making and flooring as it is tough, durable and has a beautiful grain.

Swamp Oak (*Casuarina glauca*) male flower.

Casuarina female flowers and cones.

# How are Casuarinas identified?

In general, it is not easy to distinguish between different species of Casuarinas, as the outward appearance of trees is often very similar. A magnifying glass for closer inspection of plant characteristics is normally needed for identification. The number and shape of tiny tooth-like leaves are vital in the recognition of different species. They are arranged in a whorl and appear at intervals (internodes) along branchlets. Separate male flowers emerge at the end of branchlets, whereas reddish female flowers are packed into tight heads, which after pollination develop into a woody cone. The opening valves of the cone release the fruit, a seed enclosed in a papery wing, called a samara. The size and form of the woody cone are important features in classification.

# Beach She-oak *Casuarina equisetifolia*

Under ideal conditions the Beach or Coast She-oak is a medium-sized tree able to reach a height of 20m. Trees growing on exposed sites close to the beach are normally smaller with a crooked, windblown trunk. They often develop a distinctive rounded crown with beautiful weeping foliage. This species has a very wide distribution range along Australia's coastline and is able to grow on pure sands. Bark is brown, weathering to grey and has a hard and fissured texture on mature specimens; bark on younger trees is more grey and has a smoother texture. Plantings of this species have been successful in the protection and containment of dune erosion.

The woody cone shows pronounced sharply pointed valve tips and measures up to 20mm long and 15mm in diameter. Numerous valves open to disperse the winged seeds, which are dark brown and can reach up to 8mm long. Branchlets which are needle-like at less than 1mm in diameter can reach 30cm or more long and under closer inspection show a cover of fine whitish hair. The pointed teeth-like leaves are minute at less than 1mm long, and arranged in a whorl of 7–8 at internodes up to 13mm apart. A magnifying glass is needed to observe them. Distribution: New South Wales, Queensland and Northern Territory.

# River She-oak *Casuarina cunninghamiana*

The River She-oak is a medium to tall tree growing up to 40m high which is commonly found along freshwater river systems on most of Australia's east coast. Bark is dark grey or sometimes more brown with a furrowed, rough and hard texture. The small woody cone is rounded with flattened ends or more cylindrical in shape. It measures up to 10mm in diameter and 15mm long. Every fertile cone produces a large number of winged seeds, which are brown and up to 4mm long. Thin branchlets are only up to 0.7mm in diameter and reach 25cm long. The 8–10 tiny scale-like leaves are less than 0.5mm long and appear at internodes spaced less than 1cm apart. Distribution: New South Wales, Queensland and Northern Territory.

## Desert Oak *Allocasuarina decaisneana*

The aptly named Desert Oak is frequently the dominant tree species in large areas of Australia's arid centre. Its extensive and deep root-system is able to reach underground water sources inaccessible to other trees. Under ideal conditions it can reach up to 20m high with the bushy and needle-like foliage creating its distinctive shape (habit). Bark is rough and vertically furrowed; natural colour is light brown, but trunks on mature trees often blackened by fires. The woody cone is cylindrical and measures up to 7cm long, the largest fruit produced by any member of the Casuarina family. Branchlets are needle-like at less than 1mm in diameter and can reach 30cm or more in length. Pointed teeth-like leaves are minuscule at less than 1mm long, and arranged in a whorl of 4–5 at widely spaced internodes set up to 3cm apart. Distribution: Western Australia, South Australia and Northern Territory.

# Black She-oak *Allocasuarina littoralis*

This very hardy tree has adapted to all different climate zones in Australia, ranging from the tropical north to the cool temperate climate of Tasmania. It is a small to medium-sized tree reaching up to 15m high and prefers better-drained coastal areas than the similar Swamp Oak (*Casuarina glauca*). The habitat of the Black She-oak extends inland to the higher tablelands and in some places as far as the western slopes. The deeply furrowed bark is distinctive and differentiates this species from the closely related Beach She-oak (*Casuarina equisetifolia*). The unisex flowers of this species have either male or female reproductive organs only, which frequently appear on separate trees (dioecious). The cylindrical woody cone reaches up to 4cm long and 2cm in diameter. Needle-like branchlets are less than 1mm in diameter and show 6–8 miniscule leaves. Distribution: Tasmania, Victoria, New South Wales and Queensland.

# Forest Oak *Allocasuarina torulosa*

Tall Eucalypt forests along Australia's east coast are the natural habitat of this common species. Under favourable conditions it can grow up to 25m, but as an understorey tree or in dry habitats it may only reach half that height. Even on juvenile trees the deeply furrowed bark is very evident, giving the species some fire resistance. It is brown and can be brittle to soft corky in texture. Forest Oaks produce either female or male flowers on separate trees (dioecious). The female tree alone produces the oblong woody cone which is up to 3cm long. Angular branchlets holding the miniscule leaves are up to 15cm long, less than 0.5mm in diameter, delicate, soft in texture and dark green. Only four microscopic leaves appear at internodes spaced at 5–7mm intervals. Distribution: New South Wales and Queensland.

# THE AUSTRALIAN
# RAINFORESTS

# What are Rainforests?

Australian rainforests are unique, have an ancient history and contain the highest diversity of plant life found in any forest type. They are complex ecosystems with birds, animals, insects and rainforests dependent on each other.
Rainforests occur in the Top End, from Queensland down along the East Coast to Victoria, and also in Tasmania. Today only 0.1 per cent of the Australian continent is still covered in rainforests. Until now there is no standard of rainforest classification on a nationwide level. But in general the following benchmarks are applied when identifying rainforests.

Wompoo Fruit-Dove (*Ptilinopus magnificus*).

Rainforest Bangalow Palms (*Archontophoenix cunninghamiana*).

# How are Rainforests identified?

An annual rainfall above 1,000mm is needed, but microclimates and permanent watercourses play a role. On average the density of the canopy has to be more than 70 per cent, a closed forest. Under these shady conditions the seed of Eucalyptus trees and other non-rainforest species will not geminate or develop. There shouldn't be any evidence of previous fires, as rainforest trees have little or no resistance to bush fires. Boundaries between burnt an unburnt areas can become obvious by looking around for charred trunks and logs on the ground. The resident tree species found in the forest and also the presence of other plants such as vines, palms and epiphytes (plants that grow on trees) are important factors. Finally, the soil plays a vital part in the distribution of rainforests. Often luxurious rainforests grow on rich volcanic soils.

# What are Rainforest Types?

In Australia four major kinds of rainforests are recognised, classified as tropical, subtropical, warm and cool temperate, depending on climate zones.

Tropical Rainforest has the highest diversity of trees and shrubs found in any Australian forest. A dense understorey of palms and climbing vines is typical. Smaller trees form one or two additional canopy layers (strata) beneath that of the taller trees.

In Subtropical Rainforests the number of tree species is reduced to between 60–100. Trees often have large buttress root systems and vines and palms are still present. Smaller trees and shrubs form one or two additional canopy layers.

In Warm Temperate Rainforests the diversity of trees is diminished to less than ten different and often dominant species. Large vines are absent and trees only have small buttress roots. The only palm species present is the small Walking Stick Palm (*Linospadix monostachya*).

In Cool Temperate Rainforests only two or three dominant tree species create the single layer canopy of the forest. Mosses, especially on tree trunks and understorey ferns are prominent, whereas palms and vines are absent.

# What are Rainforest Trees and Shrubs?

Rainforest species have a low resistance to bush fires, occur in high rainfall areas, and have the ability to germinate and develop under very low light conditions. Some trees occur in all types of rainforests, whereas others are restricted to a certain kind(s). This section includes trees from tropical to cool temperate climates with a focus on important families and genera. Species were chosen for their representative characteristics, abundance and wide distribution.

## Banana Bush *Tabernaemontana pandacaqui*
## Family APOCYNACEAE

The name Banana Bush refers to the bright yellow banana-shaped fruit produced by this understorey shrub. Its natural home is tropical, subtropical and warm temperate rainforest, where it can achieve a height of 3m. The bark on older stems is light brown with a finely rough texture. Stems, twigs and leaf stalks all exude a milky sap when broken, which is a good identification characteristic and a distinctive feature for members of this family. Scented flowers form into a yellowish tube at the base,

and a whorl of five pure white petals at the apex. The very ornamental fruit (a follicle) measures up to 5cm long and splits at one side only to expose seeds covered in a sticky bright red pulp. The fruit of APOCYNACEAE species is often poisonous. Simple leaves are up to 12cm long, reverse lance-shaped with wavy margins, hairless, glossy, soft and smooth in texture. Despite its decorative appearance, the poisonous fruit makes this shrub unsuitable for suburban gardens. Distribution: New South Wales and Queensland.

# Celery Wood *Polyscias elegans* Family ARALIACEAE

The bark of this medium-sized tree emits a celery-like odour when rubbed, hence the name of Celery Wood. It is distinguished by its elegant foliage, consisting of large compound leaves forming an umbrella-like shape at the end of branches. Small purple flowers are held on multi-branching stalks (panicles). The fruit (a drupe) changes to nearly black when fully ripe and measures about 5mm in diameter. Members of the genus *Polyscias* feature a large compound leaf which is divided into numerous separate leaflets arranged along a common axis (pinnate). Compound leaves of the Celery Wood can dissect even further (bipinnate) and consist of more than 50 leaflets, which are up to 12cm long, mostly egg-shaped with entire margins, celery-like scented and smooth in texture. Distribution: New South Wales and Queensland. Other well-known members of this family include the Pencil Cedar (*Polyscias murrayi*) and the Umbrella Tree (*Schefflera actinophylla*).

# Yellow Sassafras *Doryphora sassafras*
## Family ATHEROSPERMATACEAE

The Yellow Sassafras is a tall tree able to reach more than 40m in height. This and the similar Southern Sassafras (*Atherosperma moschatum*) are often dominant species in temperate rainforests. Simple leaves with toothed margins and an opposite leaf arrangement are typical features for this family. Bark is greyish-brown with a finely rough texture. Up to three white flowers are supported by a common stalk and measure up to 2.5cm across when fully opened. The small and dry fruit (an achene) consists of a single seed attached to a hairy stem (axis) up to 15mm long. Simple leaves are up to 10cm long, mostly elliptic with toothed wavy margins, leathery in texture and emit a spicy aroma when crushed. Distribution: New South Wales and Queensland; Southern Sassafras (*A. moschatum*) Tasmania, Victoria and New South Wales.

## Family CAPPARACEAE

Trees, shrubs and climbers of the genus *Capparis* are known as Caper Berries, because flowers and the fruit pulp of some species are edible. They occur in subtropical and tropical (monsoonal) rainforests, but others are also found in drier regions of all Australian states.

## Brush Caper Berry *Capparis arborea*

The habitat of the Brush Caper Berry is subtropical rainforest, where it can attain a height of up to 10m. Bark on the main trunk of mature trees is firm and rather rough in texture showing fine fissures (cracks). The trunk and branches are covered with scattered sharp spines up to 2cm long. Over summer showy

flowers supported by long individual stalks emerge from leaf axils along the younger branches. They measure up to 4cm in diameter and display four pure white petals and prominent stamens more than 3cm long. The large fruit (a berry) can reach up to 6cm in diameter and together with its elongated stalk is a common characteristic for the genus. When fully ripe the fruit becomes soft and turns yellowish-green. It contains numerous brown seeds embedded in a white pulp. Simple leaves with an alternate arrangement are up to 12cm long, ovate to broadly elliptic with entire in-rolled margins, dark green, very glossy, firm and smooth in texture. Distribution: central New South Wales to northern Queensland.

## Family COMBRETACEAE Genus *Terminalia*

# What is an Almond or Damson Tree?

About 100 *Terminalia* species exist within warmer regions of the world; of these 25 naturally occur in Australia. Trees of this genus are widespread in the tropical north of Australia and are commonly referred to as Almond trees or Damsons for their plum-like fruit. These medium to tall trees are deciduous and can develop large buttress roots such as the Damson Plum (*T. sericocarpa*).

## Australian Almond (Mueller's Damson) *Terminalia muelleri*

In its natural habitat of monsoonal rainforests this tree can reach a height of about 20m. It is semi or fully deciduous at the end of spring, with most leaves turning reddish-brown before falling. Bark on large buttress roots and on the base of trunks is hard and tessellated (scaly) and greyish-brown. The fleshy fruit (a drupe) is ovoid and measures up to 20mm long. When fully mature the fruit has a smooth and shiny surface, is hairless and dark blue. It contains a single hard, cream to orange-coloured seed reaching 12mm long. Simple leaves with an alternate arrangement are up to 12cm long, reverse egg-shaped (obovate) with a rounded apex, dark green on top, rather dull, strong and firm in texture. Two swellings (glands) typical for the genus are located at the base of the leaf blade (lamina), but are not present on all leaves. Distribution: north Queensland.

## Family CUNONIACEAE

# How are members of this family distinguished?

Members of this family are prevalent in all rainforest types on Australia's east coast and in Tasmania. The name Marara is used for a number of trees belonging to different genera of this family. Many species are distinguished by leaf-like structures called stipules, which either fall off, leaving a scar on the stem or are retained at the leaf joint. Leaves often feature serrated margins but size and shape do vary. Some species such as Red Carabeen (*Geissois benthamii*) and Coachwood (*Ceratopetalum apetalum*) are valuable timber trees.

## Rose-leaved Marara (Soft Corkwood) *Ackama paniculata*
## Family CUNONIACEAE

Masses of white to cream flowers make this tree a stand-out feature over the summer months. It can attain 30m in height and is widespread in different types of rainforests and regenerating forests alike. The distinctive bark has some variations from shallow to more deeply furrowed (grooved), but is always very soft and corky to the touch. The fruit is a tiny roundish and hairy capsule, only measuring up to 3mm long. It is reddish-brown and contains numerous very fine seeds. Compound (pinnate) leaves feature up to seven leaflets, which are up to 12cm long, mostly elliptic with finely toothed to nearly smooth margins, hairless to very hairy and rather soft in texture. Obvious stipule scars present at leaf nodes are typical for the family. Distribution: New South Wales to north Queensland.

## Davidson's Plum *Davidsonia jerseyana* Family CUNONIACEAE

This small tree has become a popular bush tucker food, being made into sauces and jams. The Davidson's Plum while often planted for its edible fruit, is uncommon in its habitat of subtropical rainforests. It is a small tree with a slender trunk, which is only sparsely branched at the top of older trees. Bark is brown with a soft and scaly texture. Clusters of pinkish red flowers are borne on the trunk or appear along branches. The sour but palatable fruit (a drupe) varies from pear- to more egg-shaped and can reach up to 5cm long. The large compound leaf shows distinctive toothed stipules at the base. It consists of 15 or more leaflets, which are up to 30cm long, oblong with toothed margins, prickly hairy and firm in texture. This genus, consisting of three species, was a recent addition to this family. Distribution: Northern Rivers, New South Wales.

## Red Carabeen *Geissois benthamii* Family CUNONIACEAE

The bright pink to vivid red colours of new leaf-growth are a distinct feature of this valuable timber tree. It reaches a height of 40m and occurs naturally in subtropical and warm temperate rainforests. Older specimens develop beautifully fluted and

buttressed trunks with a fairly smooth, reddish brown bark. Very attractive flower sprays (racemes), holding numerous white to pale yellow flowers, are up to 20cm long. The fruit is an elongated and hairy capsule measuring up to 20mm long. Splitting into two segments (valves) it disperses a number of flattened brown seeds enclosed in a small papery wing. The large and leafy stipules at the base of the leaf stalk are a distinctive characteristic of the Red Carabeen. Compound leaves consist of three leaflets (trifoliate). Leaflets are up to 20cm long, elliptic with toothed margins, hairless, glossy and rather firm. Distribution: New South Wales and Queensland.

## Family ELAEOCARPACEAE

# What are Quandong and Carabeen Trees?

The best-known trees of this family are the Quandongs (*Elaeocarpus sp.*) and the Carabeens (*Sloanea sp.*). These genera include very tall and impressive trees, which often develop massive buttress roots. Members of this family are found in tropical to temperate rainforests stretching from Tasmania to northern Australia. Common characteristics for the Quandongs (*Elaeocarpus* sp.) are the often blue-coloured fruits, containing a hard grooved stone, and simple leaves with mostly serrated margins.

## Blue Quandong (Silver Quandong) *Elaeocarpus grandis*
## Family ELAEOCARPACEAE

Mature Blue Quandong trees are uncommon nowadays as the timber is a valuable resource. In subtropical and tropical rainforests it is a tall tree attaining more than 40m in height with a straight upright trunk and large buttress roots. The distinctive bark is light grey, smooth and firm in texture. Small whitish flowers are bell-shaped with five frilled petals, blooming over autumn and winter.

The typical rounded blue fruit (a drupe) is fleshy and up to 25mm in diameter, containing a deeply grooved and very hard stone. Alternately arranged simple leaves are up to 16cm long, oblong with finely toothed margins, hairless, glossy on both surfaces, strong and firm in texture. Older leaves will often turn red before falling. The strong leaf stalk can measure up to 25mm long. Several swellings (domatia) along the centre vein are very evident. Distribution: northern New South Wales to northern Queensland.

## Blueberry Ash (Blue Olive Berry) *Elaeocarpus reticulatus* Family ELAEOCARPACEAE

This widespread and eye-catching small to medium-sized tree reaches a height of up to 20m. It is found in rainforests and a variety of other forest types where it prefers locations along riverbanks. Bark colour varies from brown to dark grey with a firm and finely rough texture. Masses of fragrant pure white flowers are characteristically bell-shaped with fringed petals. Flowers emerge in early spring in warmer regions and late spring to summer in cooler climates. The beautiful small blue fruit (a drupe) resembles a blueberry and measures about 1cm long. It contains a single very hard and grooved seed. Simple leaves with an alternate arrangement are up to 12cm long, elliptical to reverse lance-shaped with finely toothed margins, strong and firm in texture. Distribution: Tasmania, Victoria, New South Wales and southern Queensland.

## Yellow Carabeen *Sloanea woollsii* Family ELAEOCARPACEAE

Within subtropical rainforests this majestic large tree can grow up to 60m high, but it has been extensively logged for its valuable timber. It is closely related to the White Carabeen (*S. langii*) prevalent within tropical rainforests, but not to the Red Carabeen (*Geissois benthamii*), which belongs to a different family. Older trees develop distinctive sail-like buttress roots reaching far up the trunk. Bark is grey and rather smooth in texture. White flowers held on individual stalks are attached to a spike (a raceme) and bloom over spring. The fruit is a spiky capsule opening into two chambers (valves) each containing one seed, which is covered in a yellow or reddish skin (aril). Simple leaves with an alternate arrangement are up to 16cm long, broadly elliptic to reverse lance-shaped with toothed margins, strong and firm in texture. Distribution: northern New South Wales to central Queensland.

## Pea and Bean Family FABACEAE (Subfamily FABOIDEAE)

# What have Members of this Family in common?

Members of the Pea and Bean family (FABACEAE) are legumes, which all have the ability to extract nitrogen from the atmosphere and enrich poor soil. In Australia the subfamily FABOIDEAE contains a large number of shrubs, but only few species that will reach tree size. Being legumes these shrubs often play an important role in the development of forests growing on nutrient-deficient soils. Characteristic flowers are made up of a large petal at the top called a standard, two side petals referred to as wings, and the keel two fused petals at the base.

## Black Bean *Castanospermum australe*
## Family FABACEAE (Subfamily FABOIDEAE)

The ornamental Black Bean is often planted as a street tree and grown in forest plantations for its valuable timber. In its natural habitat of subtropical and tropical rainforests it is able to attain 40m in height. Bark is greyish-brown with a finely rough and firm texture. Splendid flowers with orange to red petals and a yellow base (calyx) are up to 5cm long. The fruit develops into

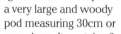

a very large and woody pod measuring 30cm or more long. It contains 2–6 large rounded and brown seeds up to 5cm long. Seeds are poisonous to livestock and humans. Compound leaves are up to 35cm long and consist of 7–19 large leaflets, which are up to 17cm long, lance-shaped with entire margins, glossy, firm and smooth in texture. Distribution: north coast of New South Wales to north Queensland.

## Pea and Bean Family FABACEAE (Subfamily MIMOSOIDEAE)

This subfamily also includes all Wattle trees (*Acacia* sp.), of which only a limited number inhabit rainforests.

### Pink Lace Flower (Fairy Paint Brush) *Archidendron grandiflorum* MIMOSOIDEAE

The stunning and fragrant flowers unfold their white petals to reveal a bundle of dark pink stamens, giving meaning to the name of Fairy Paint Brush. This small tree attains a height of 15m and prefers shaded positions under a canopy of taller trees. It is found within warm temperate, subtropical and tropical rainforests. Bark is brown and becomes rough, furrowed and scaly on older trees. The remarkable fruit (a pod) is either spiral-shaped reaching up to 8cm in diameter, or twisted and able to reach 20cm long. It splits open to reveal a vivid red inside surface and up to 12 black and very shiny seeds. The compound (bipinnate) leaf features up to four pairs of stems (pinnae) which join the primary leaf stalk and hold 4–8 leaflets each. Leaflets are between 3–8cm long, elliptic to broadly lance-shaped with entire broadly undulating margins, mostly hairless, dark green and glossy on top, thin, papery but rather strong in texture. Distribution: New South Wales

to northern Queensland. The White Lace Flower (*A. hendersonii*) is very similar in appearance, but differs in that flower stamens are pure white and fewer leaflets are present. Both species make excellent ornamental plants for sheltered positions.

## The Laurels Family LAURACEAE

# What have Laurel Trees in common?

Members of this family are well represented in most rainforest types existing in Australia. There are more than 100 species in nine genera varying in size from small to tall trees. The family is of ancient origin with fossil records in Australia dating back to more than 80 million years ago. The term Walnut is included in the common names of many species and the name Sassafras relates to the spicy aroma of leaves. Common traits include a simple leaf with entire margins and a fleshy, often black fruit.

## Jackwood (Native Laurel) *Cryptocarya glaucescens* Family LAURACEAE

The dense foliage of the native Jackwood bears a resemblance to that of the introduced and noxious (harmful) Camphor Laurel (*Cinnamomum camphora*). It is a medium to tall tree able to attain a height of more than 30m. The Jackwood is common in different

rainforest types and often encountered as a pioneer tree in re-growth areas. Bark is brown with a firm, rough and sometimes scaly texture. Small and inconspicuous flowers are cream to light brown and blossom over spring. The fleshy fruit (a drupe) changes from green to glossy black with maturity and measures up to 15mm across. Simple leaves typical for the genus are up to 12cm long, elliptic to oblong with entire margins, mostly hairless, glossy, even or blotchy grey-green beneath, camphor scented, thick and strong in texture. Distribution: New South Wales to northern Queensland.

## Pink Walnut (Hard Corkwood) *Endiandra sieberi*
## Family LAURACEAE

Coastal (littoral) rainforests and occasionally upland subtropical rainforests are the habitats of this medium-sized tree. Compared to other rainforest species, the Pink Walnut has some fire resistance due to the nature of its protective bark. It is deeply furrowed with a fairly firm but corky texture. Flowers are borne on multi-branching stalks (a panicle) emerging over winter and early spring. They measure 5–7mm in diameter with six rounded, white to cream-coloured petals. The fleshy fruit (a drupe) is shiny black and reaches up to 3cm long. It is shaped like an olive and contains a single hard seed. Simple fragrant leaves with an alternate arrangement are up to 10cm long, elongated elliptic with entire margins, dark green and glossy on top, hairless, smooth and rather leathery in texture. Distribution: New South Wales south coast to Queensland.

## Oliver's Sassafras (Camphorwood) *Cinnamomum oliveri*
## Family LAURACEAE

The bark and leaves of this tree emit a pleasant spicy aroma when rubbed or crushed, thereby making it relatively easy to identify. It is a widespread medium to tall tree growing in different rainforests types along Australia's east coast. The light brown bark on mature trees is firm and relatively smooth in texture, although some softer blisters can be present. Scented flowers are held on multi-branching stalks (panicles) and bloom over spring. The fruit is an olive-shaped drupe sitting in a cup-shaped base. It turns black when fully mature and reaches up 15mm long. Simple leaves of this genus have an opposite arrangement (sometimes slightly offset), compared to the regular alternate arrangement of other genera in this family. They are up to 16cm long, lance-shaped with entire wavy margins, firm, leathery and emit a strong sassafras scent when crushed. Distribution: New South Wales south coast to northern Queensland.

## The Mallows Family MALVACEAE

# What are Mallows?

In Australia shrub- or tree-sized members of this diverse family play an integral part in the composition of subtropical and tropical rainforests. There are 26 genera with more than 150 species native to Australia, with the majority of them being short-lived plants (herbs). The popular native Hibiscus shrubs and the beautiful flowering Kurrajongs belong to this family.

## Blush Tulip Oak (Booyong) *Argyrodendron actinophyllum*
## Family MALVACEAE

The Blush Tulip Oak (*A. actinophyllum*) and its close relatives the Red and Brown Tulip Oak (*A. peralatum* and *A.trifoliolatum*) are impressive rainforest giants over 50m high. Massive trunks with extensive buttress roots and a rough scaly bark are characteristic traits. The typical fruit is a seed enclosed in a dry and papery wing (a samara). The samara can reach up to 6cm long and appear single, joined in pairs or in small groups. The characteristic compound leaf is divided into separate leaflets joining the primary leaf stalk at a central point (palmate). The Brown (*A. trifoliolatum*) and Red Tulip Oak (*A. peralatum*) have three leaflets; whereas the Blush Tulip Oak (*A. actinophyllum*) can have up to nine leaflets. Leaflets of the Blush Tulip Oak are up to 18cm long, lance-shaped or elliptical,

dark green on top and paler green below. Leaflets of the Brown Tulip Oak are silvery on the underside, and copper-coloured for the Red Tulip Oak. Distribution: New South Wales to northern Queensland.

## Pink Hibiscus *Hibiscus splendens* Family MALVACEAE

This gorgeous native shrub grows to a height of 4m and naturally prefers transition zones between rainforests and tall open forests. The Pink Hibiscus (Hibiscus splendens) and the closely related Native Rosella (Hibiscus heterophyllus) make excellent additions to any garden, as they are known for their long-lasting and striking flowers. The Pink Hibiscus features pink flowers compared to white with pink fringes for the Native Rosella. They both have dark crimson centres and can reach up to 8cm in diameter. The pointed, egg-shaped fruit (a capsule) becomes woody and is covered in bristly whitish hair. Simple leaves of the Pink Hibiscus are up to 18cm long with finely toothed margins, varied in shape from deeply lobed to broadly lance-shaped, dark green, with whitish hair and a few small prickles. Distribution: New South Wales to northern Queensland. Most of the 35 native species of Hibiscus in Australia are found on the east coast.

## Flame Tree (Flame Kurrajong) *Brachychiton acerifolius* Family MALVACEAE

The Flame Tree is well known and often planted as an ornamental for its splendid flowers. Originating in warmer types of rainforests, it attains a height of 35m and is deciduous or semi-deciduous for a short time in spring. The vivid red flower display of mature trees is intensified by the absence of any leaves. Bell-shaped flowers reach about 1cm in diameter, supported by flower stalks which are also bright red. The typical fruit for the genus is a hard and boat-shaped follicle containing rows of tightly packed seeds. These are enclosed in a thin and papery layer which is hairy and can cause irritation to the skin. Simple leaves show an alternate arrangement and are up to 25cm long, deeply lobed to oblong or egg-shaped, hairless, mid-green, glossy, thick and firm in texture.

## Family MELIACEAE

# What do Members of this Family have in common?

This family includes iconic rainforest trees such as Red Cedar (*Toona ciliata*) and Rosewood (*Dysoxylum fraserianum*). In Australia the genus *Dysoxylum* has the largest number of species (15) in the family MELIACEAE, with a distribution range covering all states except Victoria and Tasmania. Most of the other 10 Australian genera in this relatively small family contain a single or only a few species. A compound leaf with eight to more than 20 separate leaflets is characteristic for most genera in this family.

## Red Cedar *Toona ciliata* Family MELIACEAE

Found in different types of rainforests, this magnificent large tree is able to reach a height of more than 50m.

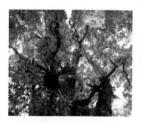

Old trees support a multitude of epiphytes (plants growing on trees) and develop an expansive buttress root-system. Extensive logging for its beautiful and valuable timber since the early 1830s has made mature specimens a rarity nowadays. Bark is light

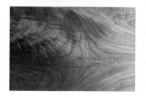

brown, scaly and rough, flaky in texture. Small whitish flowers are held on drooping multi-branching stalks (a panicle). The pear-shaped fruit (a capsule) is up to 20mm long, splitting into five segments (valves) containing tightly packed winged seeds. After a short deciduous time over winter, new emerging foliage often flushes in red tones. Compound leaves consist of up to 20 leaflets which are up to 14cm long, mostly egg-shaped with entire margins, hairless, smooth and rather soft in texture. Small hairy swellings (domatia) along the centre vein are obvious. Distribution: New South Wales to northern Queensland.

# Rosewood (Rose Mahogany) *Dysoxylum fraserianum*
# Family MELIACEAE

The common name Rosewood is a reference to the pleasant smell released when the bark or tree is cut. It is a valuable timber tree, able to attain more than 50m in height with a massive trunk up to 3m in diameter. Due to logging mature trees have become increasingly rare in their natural habitat of subtropical rainforests. Bark is light brown and has a rough scaly texture. Small flowers are scented and cream to pale mauve. The roughly rounded fruit (a capsule) measures up to 4cm in diameter and splits open into 3–4 segments (valves). The distinctive compound leaf (pinnate) consists of 4–12 leaflets, which are up to 12cm long, mainly lance-shaped with entire margins, rather soft and smooth in texture. Prominent swellings (domatia) along the mid-vein of the leaflets are a reliable identification feature. Distribution: New South Wales to southern Queensland.

## White Cedar *Melia azedarach* Family MELIACEAE

This very adaptable species is often used as a shade or street tree in many parts of Australia, even in dry and arid regions. It is deciduous over winter with vibrant green new foliage appearing in early spring. Under ideal conditions it can grow to more than 30m high and naturally occurs in different rainforests types and drier open forests. Bark is grey, brown and white with a hard and fissured texture. Fragrant flowers, appearing in spring, are mauve and white. The olive-shaped and fleshy fruit (a drupe) turns yellow when fully ripe and is poisonous to humans and livestock. Do not place water troughs for animals under or near this tree. The large compound leaf can consist of more than 70 small leaflets, which are up to 5cm long, mostly egg-shaped with toothed or entire margins, thin and fairly soft. Distribution: New South Wales, Queensland, Northern Territory and Western Australia.

## The Fig Trees, Genus *Ficus* Family MORACEAE

# What are Fig Trees?

Fig trees are often impressive tall trees with a wide canopy and a large spreading buttress root-system. There are about 40 different species found in Australia with a natural distribution ranging from the tropical north including Western Australia down to Victoria. Figs trees favour areas receiving high rainfall or grow near permanent watercourses. All figs play an important role in a forest's ecosystem, as they are a staple food source for many birds, fruit bats and other animals. The diversity of other rainforest tree species around and under old fig trees is immense, as birds and bats bring in seeds from far and wide. The most spectacular trees are the Strangler Figs, which start life high up in a host tree and with a network of roots entangle and finally kill it. Some fig trees can live for more than 1,000 years and are the centrepiece of many large public gardens.

Top: Inside of Strangler Fig (*Ficus watkinsiana*).
Bottom: Moreton Bay Fig (*Ficus macrophylla*) leaves.

# How are Fig Trees recognised?

When a leaf stalk or young stem is broken a white or clear sap (liquid) will seep from the cut. On contact with the air this sap turns sticky very quickly and can irritate eyes and skin when touched. Emerging leaves are protected by two sheaves called stipules, which fall of before the leaf unfurls and leave behind a scar on the stem. Leaves are held in an alternate arrangement and are often thick and leathery or have a rough sandpapery surface. The fleshy fruit, a fig, can be dark blue, red or yellow and contains a large number of small seeds. Most Australian figs are edible, but with some exceptions are normally not very palatable.

## Creek Sandpaper Fig *Ficus coronata* Family MORACEAE

This small to medium-sized tree mainly grows along watercourses and in different types of rainforests. Buttress roots can develop on older trees to support the spreading crown. The Creek Sandpaper Fig does not have a strangling habit. Grey to brown bark is fairly smooth to finely rough in texture. The reverse egg-shaped fig is up to 2.5cm long, hairy and dark purple to nearly black when fully ripe. The edible fruit can also appear on older trunks and is sweet and palatable after the hairy skin has been removed. Simple leaves are up to 12cm long, oblong or egg-shaped with irregular finely toothed to nearly entire margins, dark green, hairy beneath and sandpaper like in texture. Stipules are up to 12mm long. The leaf stalk is 15mm long and exudes clear sap when broken. Distribution: Victoria, New South Wales, Queensland, Northern Territory and Western Australia.

## Curtain Fig (White Fig) *Ficus virens var. sublanceolata* Family MORACEAE

The impressive Curtain Fig has a strong strangling habit and can develop into a very large tree able to reach 50m in height when overgrowing other tall rainforest trees. Subtropical and tropical rainforests are its natural habitat. Bark is firm and rather smooth with some bumps and ridges; colour is a light to medium grey. The pink or whitish fig measures up to 12mm in diameter, is globe-shaped and supported by a very short stalk arising from the leaf axils. Simple leaves with an alternate arrangement are up to 15cm long, oblong or lance-shaped with entire margins, dark green, glossy above, lighter green beneath, smooth and thinner than species such as the Moreton Bay or Strangler Fig. The leaf stalk exudes a sticky white sap when cut or broken and reaches up to 6cm long. Stipules are up to 15mm long. Distribution: New South Wales, Queensland, Northern Territory and Western Australia.

## Moreton Bay Fig *Ficus macrophylla* Family MORACEAE

The massive and very long-lived Moreton Bay Fig can attain a height of 50m, but even more imposing is the diameter of the spreading crown. It prefers moist and rich soils, often growing close to watercourses and within different rainforest types. Older specimens feature short but enormous trunks with buttress roots extending above ground for many metres. Bark is shades of grey, rough and dry in texture. Figs change to a deep purple, speckled with white or yellow dots, when fully ripe and measure up to 30mm in diameter. Simple leaves are up to 25cm long, broadly oblong to egg-shaped with entire margins, hairless, glossy, dark green on top, brownish on their underside, thick and leathery in texture. Leaf stalks are up to 10cm long and exude a sticky white sap when broken. Large stipules are up to 15cm long. Distribution: New South Wales and Queensland.

## Rusty Fig (Port Jackson Fig) *Ficus rubiginosa* Family MORACEAE

The Rusty Fig is one of a limited number of species with a natural distribution range reaching as far south as Victoria. It can grow up to 25m tall and develop a wide spreading canopy. The light grey bark has a firm texture and shows small horizontal ridges. The globe-shaped fig is held on a stiff stalk and measures up to 2cm in diameter. Fruit appears in late summer to autumn and changes from orange to red with full maturity. Simple leaves with an alternate arrangement are up to 11cm long, egg-shaped or broadly elliptic with entire margins, dark green, glossy on top, paler green to rusty brown beneath, sometimes hairy, firm and leathery in texture. The strong leaf stalks are up to 4cm long and exude milky sap when broken. Stipules are up to 5cm long. Distribution: Victoria, New South Wales and Queensland.

## Small-Leaved Fig (Figwood) *Ficus obliqua* Family MORACEAE

Under ideal conditions this very large fig tree with a strangling habit is able to reach a height of 50m. Older trees develop a very substantial trunk with far-reaching buttress roots. Bark is firm in texture, grey and marked by small, irregular horizontal ridges. The rounded fruit is relatively small for an Australian fig at only 10mm in diameter, and turns from yellow to orange or red when fully ripe. Simple leaves are only up to 8cm long, mostly egg-shaped (ovate) with entire margins, dark green, glossy, firm, smooth in texture, but not as leathery and thick as other fig leaves. Leaf stalk exudes a sticky white sap when cut or broken and reaches up to 2.5cm long. Stipules protecting emerging leaves are up to 40mm long. This species makes a very good bonsai tree. Distribution: New South Wales and Queensland.

## Strangler Fig *Ficus watkinsiana* Family MORACEAE

Warmer types of rainforests are the home of this magnificent, large and very tall tree species. It has a very strong strangling habit and uses other tall rainforest trees such as Yellow Carabeen (*Sloanea woollsii*) as a host; thereby reaching more than 50m in height. Bark is grey, hard and overall rather smooth in texture. When fully ripe the large fig turns a dark purple, speckled with greenish dots. It is up to 4cm long and 2.5cm wide, oblong or more egg-shaped with a noticeable point at the top. The abundant fruit produced over late winter into spring is an important food source for many animals. Simple leaves are up to 22cm long, lance-shaped with entire margins, smooth, thick and leathery in texture. The leaf stalk is up to 8cm long and exudes a milky sap when broken. Stipules are up to 6cm long. Distribution: New South Wales and Queensland.

## Rainforest Trees in The Myrtle Family MYRTACEAE

# What are fleshy fruited Myrtles?

Eucalypts are well-known members of the diverse Myrtle family. However this family also contains many species originating in rainforests. Trees belonging to the large genus *Syzygium*, known as Lilly Pillies or Ashes, are classified as fleshy fruited Myrtles (Subfamily MYRTOIDEAE). They have a conspicuous presence in most Australian rainforest types. The Lilly Pilly (*Syzygium smithii*) and many other species in this genus are extensively used for landscaping purposes. Simple leaves with an opposite arrangement, exquisite flowers dominated by many stamens and the succulent fruits are typical characteristics.

## Powderpuff Lilly-Pilly *Syzygium wilsonii* subsp. *wilsonii*
## Family MYRTACEAE

Luxurious tropical rainforests are the original habitat of this eye-catching shrub. The Powder Puff Lilly Pilly can reach a height of 5m, competing for available sunlight under a dense rainforest canopy. As an ornamental plant, receiving more sunlight and nutrient, it will develop a compact canopy and only grow 2–3m tall. Bark is reddish-brown, firm and slightly rough in texture. Large powder-puff shaped flower-heads are formed by dense clusters of individual tubular flowers. Numerous stamens with dark pink to purple-coloured filaments, topped by white anthers, make up their striking appearance. Bunches of white and rounded or more egg-shaped fruits are produced over autumn. Simple leaves with an opposite arrangement are up to 18cm long, mostly lance-shaped with in-rolled margins, hairless, strong and slightly stiff in texture. New leaf growth flushes in different tones of pink, salmon or purple. Distribution: northern Queensland.

## Purple Cherry (Rose Satinash) *Syzygium crebrinerve* Family MYRTACEAE

Impressive buttress roots and a straight trunk are regular features of this tall tree species reaching up to 40m high. Subtropical rainforests are the exclusive habitat of the Purple Cherry. Mosses often obscure the grey-brown bark which has a firm and somewhat scaly texture. Numerous white stamens about 1cm long are the prominent feature of flowers that bloom over spring. The gorgeous shiny purple fruit (a berry) measures up to 2.5cm in diameter and matures over summer. In some years berries are produced in large quantities and can be found spread out over the forest floor. It is irregularly rounded with flattened ends (globular) and contains a single seed surrounded by an edible white fruit pulp. Simple leaves are up to 12cm long and broadly lance-shaped. Distribution: north New South Wales to central Queensland.

## Riberry *Syzygium luehmannii* Family MYRTACEAE

The Riberry is widely used in cultivation for its beautiful weeping foliage, flowers and stunning fruit display. It can attain a height of more than 30m in its subtropical and littoral (close to the beach) rainforest habitat. Bark on the trunk of older specimens is rough, fissured and reddish-brown. White flowers are tightly packed into small multi-branching heads (panicles), appearing at the very end of young branches. Flowering can occur over a long period throughout the year. The abundant red fruit is mostly pear-shaped, containing a single seed covered in whitish flesh and measures up to 15mm long. Simple leaves with an opposite arrangement are up to 6cm long, egg or broadly lance-shaped with entire and slightly incurved margins, hairless, smooth and rather firm. New leaf-growth is a stunning dark pink colour. Distribution: New South Wales mid-north coast to tropical northern Queensland.

# Rainforest Trees in The Myrtle Family MYRTACEAE

## Lemon Myrtle (Lemon Ironwood) *Backhousia citriodora*
Family MYRTACEAE

In Australia the *Backhousia* genus has several species that originate in rainforests, ranging from temperate to tropical climates. The Lemon Myrtle is probably the best-known tree belonging to this genus. In its natural habitat it is a medium-sized tree reaching up to 20m high, whereas planted in full sunlight it is a smaller tree with a dense and rounded crown. The Lemon Myrtle is known for its essential oil used in soaps, perfumes and aromatherapy. Trees are grown on large commercial plantations and as beautiful ornamentals in many gardens. Bark is a dark brown and on the trunk of older specimens becomes very rough and deeply furrowed. A beautiful and fragrant flower display takes place over spring into summer. Masses of small, individual white flowers are arranged in umbrella-shaped heads (umbels). The fruit has the appearance of a flower due to five rounded sepals (remains of the flower base) still surrounding the small capsule. It measures up to 5mm long and is divided in two longitudinal sections containing a large number of tiny seeds. Simple leaves are up to 15cm long, elliptic with finely crenate or nearly entire re-curved margins, hairless, thick, strong in texture and lemon-scented when crushed. Fragrant leaves with an opposite arrangement are characteristic for this genus. Distribution: southern to northern Queensland.

# Python Tree (Ironwood) *Gossia bidwillii* Family MYRTACEAE

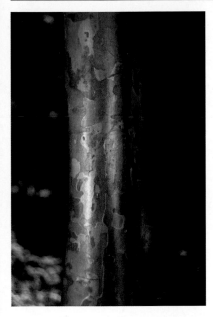

The distinctive bark makes identification of this eye-catching species rather easy. The ornamental effect is due to patches of smooth bark changing from a light to a dark green, then before shedding turning copper-brown. It is a medium-sized tree up to 20m tall and occurs in a range of different rainforest types. Up to six stalked flowers appear along a short common stalk (a raceme) up to 4cm long. Flowers typical for the genus feature rounded petals and numerous stamens all pure white. The fruit is a small berry only up to 5mm in diameter, which turns black when fully ripe. Simple leaves with an opposite arrangement are up to 10cm long, broad elliptic or egg-shaped with wavy margins, hairless, dark green, glossy, soft and polished in texture. Distribution: New South Wales and Queensland.

# Water Gum (Kanuka) *Tristaniopsis laurina* Family MYRTACEAE

This abundant and widely distributed tree prefers to grow along stream banks within all warmer rainforest types. Its hardiness and ability to stay submerged for days make this species very useful in stream bank stabilisation (re-vegetation) work below flood-level. Bark with a very smooth texture is grey, turning brown before shedding in long strips. Prolific amounts of bright yellow flowers with five small rounded petals appear in spring or summer depending on climate. The fruit (a capsule) hardens and changes to dark brown

before splitting open at the apex. Normally three separate valves (segments) contain a number of small cream-coloured seeds enclosed in a papery wing. Simple leaves with an alternate arrangement are up to 15cm long, reverse lance-shaped with entire margins, dark green, glossy, firm and leathery to the touch. Distribution: Victoria, New South Wales and Queensland.

# Antarctic Beech *Nothofagus moorei* Family NOTHOFAGACEAE

As the common name implies, ancestors of this stately tree were part of the Antarctic flora more than 80 million years ago. The Antarctic Beech and its close relative the Myrtle Beech (*N. cunninghamii*) produce an excellent timber, which has made mature specimens rare, except for older trees protected in national parks. The enchanting Antarctic Beech is a dominant species in cool temperate rainforest receiving frost and snow at higher altitudes. Huge twisted multiple trunks deeply covered in mosses are an unmistakable trademark of the Antarctic Beech. The conspicuous reddish-brown bark has a rough, scaly texture and sheds in irregularly sized plates. The hard outer-shell containing the fruit is covered in rough prickles and measures up to 8mm long. It opens into four segments (valves) containing three tiny nuts enclosed in a papery wing. The two outer nuts are ridged whereas the centre one is flattened in shape. New leaf-growth is bright red and shows obvious red tentacles (stipules) at leaf joints. Simple leaves with an alternate arrangement are up to 6cm long, mostly egg-shaped with finely toothed margins, hairless, dark green, glossy on top, paler green and dull beneath, thick and stiff in texture. Leaves on saplings and coppice shoots (off-shoots) reach 10cm or more in length. Distribution: Antarctic Beech (*N. moorei*), New South Wales to southern Queensland; Myrtle Beech (*N. cunninghamii*), Tasmania and Victoria.

## Sweet Pittosporum *Pittosporum undulatum*
## Family PITTOSPORACEAE

Abundance, broad distribution and popularity as an ornamental plant are the reasons for this shrub or small tree to be easily recognised. It is common in all different types of rainforests, tall open forests and frequently in re-growth areas. Bark is grey-brown and firm in texture. Beautiful white and sweetly scented flowers, measuring up to 20mm in diameter, have made the Sweet Pittosporum a favourite in suburban gardens. The fruit, characteristic for this genus, is a capsule up to 15mm long, containing numerous red and very sticky seeds. Simple leaves develop in a whorl arrangement, then turn alternate. Leaves are up to 15cm long, mostly elliptic with wavy margins, dark green, glossy and smooth in texture. Distribution: Victoria, New South Wales and Queensland. This species has been declared a noxious weed in areas outside its natural distribution range.

## Native Frangipani *Hymenosporum flavum*
## Family PITTOSPORACEAE

The large and stunning flowers are pure white when opening, and then change to a bright yellow with maturity. Appearing in spring, they give off a delightful fragrance and measure up to 5cm in diameter. The Native Frangipani can develop into a medium-sized tree within its natural rainforest habitat, but when growing in full sunlight it will be smaller and more compact in shape. Bark is light brown, furrowed and hard in texture. The distinctive fruit (a capsule) is brown, hairy on the outside and reaches up to 4cm long. It becomes woody before splitting to disperse numerous tightly packed and winged seeds. Simple leaves grouped in a whorl are up to 15cm long, mostly reverse lance-shaped with entire margins, dark green, glossy, thin, soft and smooth in texture. Distribution: New South Wales and Queensland.

## Rainforest Trees in The Protea Family PROTEACEAE

# What are Proteas?

Members of this family include the Banksias and Grevilleas, which prefer drier regions of the country, and are well-known for their unusual and amazing flowers. However, this family also includes many Australian rainforest species that produce incredible flowers.

### Firewheel Tree (Wheel of Fire) *Stenocarpus sinuatus* Family PROTEACEAE

Growing to a height of up to 25m this very attractive tree keeps its slender and upright habit (shape), even when planted in full sunlight. The Firewheel Tree naturally occurs within warmer rainforests types and is cultivated for its remarkable flower display. Individual flowers are a vivid red and arranged in umbrella-shaped groups (umbels) resembling spokes of a wheel. Flowering period is over summer to autumn and can last for 8–10 weeks. The ripe fruit is a hard brown follicle reaching up to 8cm long. The follicle is topped by the remaining hardened flower style, a common characteristic for this family. It takes about 12 months to mature, before splitting to disperse numerous seeds enclosed in a papery wing. Simple leaves with an alternate arrangement are up to 25cm long, varied in shape from deeply lobed to reverse egg-shaped (obovate) with wavy margins, hairless, dark green on top, paler below, glossy on both surfaces with a firm and stiff texture. Leaves on young trees can reach more than 30cm long. Distribution: northern New South Wales to northern Queensland.

## Macadamia Nut *Macadamia integrifolia* Family **PROTEACEAE**

This tree is the ancestor of today's cultivated varieties of Macadamia Nut trees that are grown in commercial plantations around the world. In its natural habitat of rainforest the Macadamia Nut may reach 20m high and is distinguished by its dense, dark green foliage. Bark is greyish-brown with a hard, finely rough texture. Appearing over late winter, the drooping flower sprays (racemes) are up to 20cm long and hold numerous small cream-coloured flowers. The well-known fruit is a rounded follicle at up to 3cm in

diameter showing a sharp protrusion at the apex. The outer husk turns brown before splitting to reveal a smooth shell containing the very palatable seed. Simple leaves are arranged in a whorl of three and are up to 20cm long, narrow oblong or reverse lance-shaped with nearly entire margins, hairless, dark green, glossy, strong and stiff in texture. Distribution: southern to northern Queensland.

## Tree Waratah (Dorrigo Oak) *Alloxylon pinnatum* Family **PROTEACEAE**

Cooler types of rainforest in mountainous locations are the exclusive habitat of the showy Tree Waratah. It attains less than 20m in height and prefers to grow under a canopy of taller trees. The finely rough bark is hard and greyish-brown. Dense clusters of individual flowers are vivid pink to deep red and form a distinctive shape called a corymb. In this flowering structure, stalks branch off at different levels but finish at a similar height.

Leaves on saplings are deeply dissected (pinnate). Simple leaves on mature trees are up to 15cm long, lance-shaped with entire margins or deeply lobed, glossy and rather stiff in texture. This beautiful tree and its close relative the Queensland Tree Waratah (*A. flammeum*) are known for their impressive flower display, but are still underrated as native garden plants. Distribution: New South Wales and Queensland.

## Family RUBIACEAE

# What have Members of this Family in common?

In Australia members of this family are mainly shrubs or small trees which are most common in tropical rainforests of northern Queensland. Simple leaves with an opposite arrangement and a fleshy fruit (a berry or drupe) are typical identification features.

## Brown Gardenia (Yellow Mangosteen)
### *Atractocarpus fitzalanii* Family RUBIACEAE

The large fragrant flowers, attractive glossy foliage, compact size and edible fruits make this native shrub an excellent garden plant. Despite being of tropical rainforest origin this species is able to tolerate light frosts and can be planted in full sunlight. It has a compact growth habit reaching a height of 4m and can be pruned to size. Bark is beige to light brown with a finely rough texture. Multi-branching stalks (panicles), appearing at the end of branches, support more than 20 superbly scented flowers. They measure up to 3cm in diameter and feature five overlapping petals, pure white in colour. Flowering period is over spring. The fleshy fruit is rounded in shape, up to 8cm in diameter and turns a yellowish green colour when mature. The edible fruit flesh

contains a large number of flattened small black seeds. Oppositely arranged simple leaves are 20cm or more long, mostly elliptic with entire margins, dark green, glossy, hairless, very smooth and firm in texture. The common name of Native Gardenia is also used for this species. Distribution: tropical east coast of Queensland.

# Native Gardenia *Atractocarpus benthamianus*
## Family RUBIACEAE

In recent times the better-known Brown Gardenia (*Atractocarpus fitzalanii*) has been sold by nurseries under the same common name, although both species deserve recognition as an attractive ornamental plant. On fertile soils the handsome Native Gardenia is a tall shrub or small tree attaining a height of 12m. Warm temperate and subtropical rainforests up to an altitude of 1,000m are the natural habitat of this understorey species. Bark is cream to light brown and becomes scaly in texture on

older trees. Up to six flower buds and 4–5 emerging leaves are enclosed by two sheaves (stipules), which are covered in very fine hair. White fragrant flowers are tubular and measure up to 1cm long; they appear in late winter and early spring. The fleshy fruit is an egg-shaped (ovoid) berry turning a yellowish-green or more orange in colour at full maturity. It reaches up to 2.5cm long and contains a number of brown seeds. Simple leaves are grouped in loose whorls of 3–5 beneath the growing bud or have an opposite arrangement. Mature leaves are up to 20cm long, elliptic or reverse lance-shaped with entire margins, glossy, hairless on top, sparsely hairy beneath, thin and soft in texture. Distribution: northern New South Wales and Queensland.

## Family SAPINDACEAE

# How are Members of this Family indentified?

Genera belonging to this large family include the well-known Tuckeroos (*Cupaniopsis* sp.) and Tamarinds (*Diploglottis* sp.). Shrubs and trees in this family are abundant in subtropical and tropical climates but are uncommon or absent in cooler rainforests types. Compound leaves consisting of two to more than 20 leaflets and a fruit (a capsule) with mostly three segments (valves) are common traits of this family.

## Native Tamarind *Diploglottis australis* Family SAPINDACEAE

The straight slender trunk and large compound leaves concentrating at end of branches give the Native Tamarind its distinctive appearance. When growing on fertile rainforests soils it can reach more than 35m high. Buttress roots will develop at the base of older trees growing on steep or unstable ground. Bark is dark brown or grey. Small flowers measuring less than 4mm in diameter feature a light brown, softly hairy base (calyx) and four white petals. In most years abundant fruit is produced which is an important food-source for a range of rainforest birds, bats and rodents. The fruit (a capsule) turns yellowish-brown and reaches up to 2cm long. It consists of 2–3 segments (valves), splitting to reveal an orange fleshy layer (aril)

that surrounds the brown seed. Large pinnate compound leaves can reach more than 1 metre long and consist of up to 16 large leaflets, which are up to 30cm long, oblong with entire margins, dull, dark green, hairy and soft with a papery texture. Distribution: New South Wales to northern Queensland.

## Tuckeroo *Cupaniopsis anacardioides* Family SAPINDACEAE

Hardiness and handsome appearance have made this species a popular choice for many landscaping purposes. Tuckeroos are frequently planted as a shade tree in public gardens, car parks and backyards. In its original habitat of coastal (littoral) rainforests this small to medium-sized tree is able to reach 20m high. Bark is light grey and fairly smooth in texture. Small cream and yellow flowers blossom over the winter months. The fruit is an orange-brown capsule measuring up to 15mm in diameter. It opens into three segments (valves) each containing a shiny black seed, which is covered in a thin, slightly fleshy, bright red layer (aril). Compound leaves consist of 3–11 leaflets, which are up to 12cm long, mostly oblong with entire margins, dark green, strong and leathery in texture. Distribution: coastal New South Wales, Queensland, Northern Territory and Western Australia.

## Tulipwood (Corduroy) *Harpullia pendula* Family SAPINDACEAE

When planted in full sunlight the Tulipwood only grows up to 10m tall, whereas it is more likely to reach 20m high in its natural rainforest habitat. Due to its attractive foliage, manageable size and decorative fruit this species is often planted as a street tree. The name Tulipwood refers to the beautiful wood grain of its durable timber. Bark is a whitish-grey with a rather rough texture. The bright orange fruit (a capsule) measures up to 40mm across and has a characteristic flat joint in between its two sections (valves or lobes), each containing a shiny black seed. New growth in the dense foliage flushes in tones of pink to pale red. The compound leaf consists of up to 10 leaflets, which are up to 14cm long, oblong or more elliptic with entire margins, dark green, rather thin and soft in texture. Distribution: northern New South Wales to northern Queensland.

## Family URTICACEAE Genus *Dendrocnide*

# What are Stinging Trees?

In Australia the Stinging Trees (*Dendrocnide* sp.), infamous for their painful sting, are probably the best-recognised trees belonging to this family. Even hairs of half decayed leaves lying on the forest floor still have a long-lasting stinging effect.

## Giant Stinging Tree *Dendrocnide excelsa* Family URTICACEAE

These exceptional trees can indeed be giants exceeding 45m in height with massive fluted trunks more than 5m in diameter. Large buttress roots can extend above ground-level for several metres. Bark is grey to light brown and corky in texture. The fleshy swollen fruit stalks are more obvious than the actual fruit, a tiny nut hanging from the expanded stalk. Leaves are up to 30cm long, rounded or more heart-shaped with toothed margins, light green and covered in needle-like hair, which have a very painful stinging effect. The Gympie Stinger (*D. moroides*) is only shrub-sized and has very similar leaves. Distribution: New South Wales and Queensland.

## Shiny-leaved Stinging Tree *Dendrocnide photinophylla*

While the stinging effect is fairly mild compared to that of the Giant Stinging Tree and the Gympie Stinger, it is still not advised to touch the leaves. The Shiny-leaved Stinging Tree can reach 20m in height and grows in a range of different rainforest types. Bark is light brown and rather soft in texture. Typical for the genus, the tiny fruits atop the swollen fleshy stalks form grape-like bunches up to 8cm long. Simple leaves are up to 15cm long, ovate with entire to toothed margins and covered in small stinging hair. Distribution: New South Wales and Queensland.

## The Pepperbushes Family WINTERACEAE

# What are Pepperbushes known for?

The spicy piquant aroma of leaves and seeds has brought the Pepperbushes (*Tasmannia sp.*) wider recognition at the dinner table. Fresh and dried leaves of some species are used to give a spicy, bush tucker flavour to a large range of dishes. Pepperbushes are understorey shrubs whose ancestors were part of temperate rainforests covering Australia 80 million years ago. Most species are found in cool temperate rainforests in Tasmania and at higher altitudes on the mainland, with the exception of the Brush Pepperbush (*T. insipida*), which is found in warmer climates.

## Dorrigo Pepperbush *Tasmannia stipitata* Family WINTERACEAE

The bright green leaves clustering at ends of vivid red branchlets give this Pepperbush its typical appearance. This eye-catching shrub grows close to 4m in height and develops a very sturdy trunk. It is found in or at margins of cool temperate rainforests within mountainous areas that receive frost and snowfall. Bark is grey-brown and firm in texture. The fruit is a dark blue or more violet-coloured berry, oblong and up to 12mm long. It contains hard black seeds which are used for their distinct spicy taste. Simple leaves are grouped in loose whorls beneath the growing bud and change to an alternate arrangement when maturing. Leaves are up to 13cm long, lance-shaped with entire margins, glossy and emit a sweet spicy aroma when crushed. Leaves and seeds for flavouring can be purchased over the internet. Distribution: New South Wales only.

PRACTICAL SECTION
IDENTIFYING TREES AND SHRUBS

# How are Shrubs and Trees identified?

Naturally the first impression when trying to identify a tree or shrub is the all over appearance of the specimen, and if not being recognised immediately, the process of matching features and elimination begins. The ability to identify native trees depends on some basic knowledge on how to recognise plant features and an understanding of a few basic botanical concepts. With some practice, observation skills will improve making it possible to differentiate between families and genera by outward appearance alone, i.e. the ability to tell a Eucalyptus from a Wattle or Fig tree. Plant (vegetative) features include leaf, flower, fruit, bark and also the size and shape of the tree (habit).

Giant Stinging Tree (*Dendrocnide excelsa*).

Using a digital camera to capture important plant characteristics for later research is a great help. As is a notebook to record location and qualities such as the texture of bark and if present the scent of leaves, bark and flowers. Include a ruler in some of your photos to document dimension and take close-up shots of samples. Leaves play an important role in identification as inherent leaf-features are plentiful and mostly unique for the same tree species. They include special traits such as hair, venation and glands. In Australia the number of semi or fully deciduous trees or shrubs is limited, therefore a very useful identification attribute in itself.

# How to use the Internet to identify Native Trees?

Digital photography and the advance of the Internet have changed the way in which trees and shrubs are identified. It is now possible to compare your digital photos of vegetative plant features with images listed on tree identification websites, such as the national and state herbaria online resources. The number of possible choices is greatly reduced if you have been able to pinpoint the family or genus of the tree in question. Your state's herbarium website will accept plant samples for identification and provides search function based on taxonomy i.e. family, genus and species classification. Herbarium website addresses of all states and the Northern Territory are listed under 'Online Resources'.

Leaf close-up.

The Australian Tropical Rainforest Plants Identification website is worth mentioning here; it is an interactive online database where results are displayed according to your input (keys) of vegetative features, and should work without installation of extra software. With a little practice, and the support of explanatory graphics provided, this resource can be utilised by beginners to plant identification. Search results display a range of colour images showing all important plant features together with detailed text descriptions and distribution ranges. An extended version containing Australia's entire flora would be ideal. A selection of online resources is supplied at the end of this guide.

# How to use Habit (Shape and Size) in Tree Identification?

In some cases attributes such as size, shape of the canopy and formation of branches are distinctive enough to identify the tree species. Furthermore shape characteristics of the trunk, which can be fluted, multi-stemmed, crooked or upright are vital in the identification of native trees and shrubs. Large buttress roots can form on Fig trees and other tall rainforest species but are small or absent on Eucalypts, Wattles or Casuarinas. The shape and height of a tree often depends on the environment and its location. For example the Beach She-oak (*Casuarina equisetifolia*) is a multi-stemmed shrub in exposed coastal positions but can reach a height of more than 20m in sheltered areas. Normally there is also a notable difference in height and shape of trees growing in full sunlight, compared to specimens competing for available daylight in a dense forest situation.

Roots of Curtain Fig (*Ficus virens*).

Fluted trunk.

# How to use Bark Features
# in Tree Identification?

Colour, texture and scent of bark are distinctive attributes which are present all year round. The different bark characteristics combined with other vegetative features such as habit and leaves play an important role in the identification of trees and shrubs. There are many ways in which trees shed their bark, ranging from long strips to rounded patches (plates) and from small scale-like flakes to thin papery layers. Detracting factors of bark identification are changes in colour and texture depending on wet or dry weather periods. In addition bark of young trees can be significantly different to that of mature specimens, and some natural variations within the same species are possible. Remember photos will not record the scent or hardness of bark.

# What are Bark Types?

1. Smooth and hard, Blue Gum (*Eucalyptus saligna*).

2. Papery and flaky, Long-leaved Paperbark (*Melaleuca leucadendra*).

3. Stringy and fibrous, Turpentine (*Syncarpia glomulifera*).

4. Soft, corky and furrowed, Rose-leaved Marara (*Ackama paniculata*).

5. Hard and furrowed, Swamp Oak (*Casuarina glauca*).

6. Scaly and rough, Pink Bloodwood (*Corymbia intermedia*).

7. Fissured and rough, White Cedar (*Melia azedarach*).

8. Finely rough or granular, Small-leaved Fig (*Ficus obliqua*).

# How to use Leaf Characteristics in Tree Identification?

### What is a Simple or Compound leaf?
The ability to distinguish between a simple and a compound leaf plays an important role in identifying any tree species.

1. A **simple leaf** is made up of a leaf stalk called a petiole and a leaf blade. A small growth bud (red circle) called an axillary bud is positioned where the leaf stalk (A) joins the young branch (B). This axillary bud can develop into a new shoot or a flowering stem. Simple leaves can have an alternate (shown) or opposite arrangement and sometimes emerge in a whorl.

2. A **compound leaf** is formed by two or more separate leaflets. The main difference is the absence of any growth (axillary) buds at the base of the leaflet stalks (A), so no new shoot or flower stem can develop from there. The graphic shows a compound leaf with four leaflets and the only growth buds (red circles) appear at joint of the common leaf stalk (B) with the young branch (C).

### Common Leaf or Leaflet Shapes

1. Straight, long and narrow (linear)
2. Straight, broader with parallel sides (oblong)
3. Oval, broadest in the middle (elliptic)
4. Egg-shaped (ovate)

5. Reverse egg-shaped (obovate)
6. Lance-shaped (lanceolate)
7. Reverse lance-shaped (oblanceolate)
8. Sickle-shaped (falcate)
9. Rounded (orbicular)

# What are different Compound Leaf Characteristics?

1. A **palmate compound leaf** has between three to more than a dozen separate leaflets, which all radiate from the apex of a common leaf stalk.

Black Booyong (*Argyrodendron actinophyllum*).

2. A **pinnate compound leaf** consists of three or more leaflets positioned on either side along a common axis (rhachis).

Native Tamarind (*Diploglottis australis*).

3. A **bipinnate compound leaf** is further divided, with pinnate leaves themselves attached to a common axis.

Red circles show position of growth (axillary) buds. Even further divided tripinnate (fern-like) compound leaves are rare on Australian trees. A bifoliate compound leaf has only two and a trifoliate only three leaflets. A compound leaf can feature more than 50 individual leaflets.

Pink Lace Flower (*Archidendron grandiflorum*).

## Basic Leaf or Leaflet Margins (Edges)
1. Smooth margins (entire)
2. Rounded teeth (crenate)
3. Sharp fine teeth (serrate)
4. Deeply indented (lobed)
5. Wavy margins (undulate)

1    2    3    4    5

# How to use Flower Characteristics in Tree Identification?

An important aspect of flowers in classification is that species of the same genus or family will bear a very similar inflorescence. Some Australian trees and shrubs produce large and colourful flowers with a long flowering period making their identification relatively easy. Flowers of most Australian trees are bisexual, meaning that male and female reproductive organs are contained in the same flower. Unisex flowers feature either male or female reproductive parts only, which can appear on the same (monoecious) or on separate trees (dioecious).

## Flower Anatomy

The male reproductive organ of a flower is called a stamen, which consists of the anther, a swollen sac containing male pollen, and the filament, the stem holding up the anther. Female reproductive parts as a unit are referred to as a carpel. It consists of a stigma receiving the pollen, which is then transferred to the ovary through a hollow tube named a style. The ovary contains egg-cells (ovules), which after fertilisation produce the seed. A flower can feature multiple carpels and the number of stamens can range from a few to more than 50. Petals don't have a reproductive function but attract pollinators. The base of a flower is called a calyx and the individual flower stalk is a pedicel.

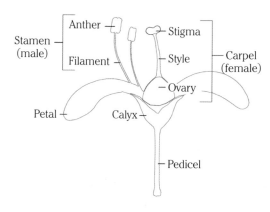

# What are Types of Flower Arrangements (Inflorescences)?

The botanical term of inflorescence refers to the whole flowering part of a plant. The primary flower stalk at the base of an inflorescence is called a peduncle. Only some Australian trees produce a solitary flower with a single stalk (peduncle) arising from leaf axils. In warmer types of rainforest flowers can also appear on the trunks of trees (cauliflorous).

A **Spike**: Flowers are attached without individual stalks (pedicels) to a single central stem.
Bottlebrush (*Callistemon* sp.).

A **Raceme**: Each flower is attached by its own stalk (pedicel) to a single central axis (rhachis).
Red Carabeen (*Geissois benthamii*).

A **Panicle**: Flowers are held on multi-branching stalks, which can be loosely shaped or form a dense umbrella shaped cluster.
Rose-leaved Marara (*Ackama paniculata*).

A **Corymb**: A type of inflorescence where flower stalks branch off at different levels but flowers are held at a roughly even height.
Tree Waratah (*Alloxylon pinnatum*).

# How to use Fruit Characteristics in Tree Identification?

Fruit and seeds are probably more practical than flowers in tree identification, as they are longer-lasting and can be collected beneath the tree. Fruits with a woody exterior and hard-shelled seeds will last for several months or more.

# What are different types of fruit?

**Berry**: a fleshy (succulent) fruit with only a few or many seeds, which are not released (indehiscent). The whole or part of the fruit is eaten and the seed dispersed by birds and other animals or decay on the ground.

Caper Berry *(Capparis arborea)*.

**Drupe**: a fleshy fruit that does not open (indehiscent) with one or two seeds enclosed in a hard outer layer (endocarp). The fruit, if not eaten by animals or insects, will decay quite quickly, but the seed enclosed in a hard shell is durable.

Davidson's Plum *(Davidsonia jerseyana)*.

**Follicle**: a dry fruit splitting at one side only to release a number of seeds (dehiscent). Mature follicles often become leathery or woody and after falling persist on the ground. Seeds can be enclosed in a papery wing or surrounded by a thin papery layer (aril).

Flame Tree *(Brachychiton acerifolius)*.

**Pod or Legume**: a dry fruit splitting along both sides in a lengthwise direction (dehiscent). All Wattle trees (*Acacia sp.*) produce straight or twisted pods, which develop a leathery or woody texture with full maturity. A stalk attaches the seed to the inside of the pod.

Green Wattle (*Acacia decurrens*).

**Capsule**: a dry fruit consisting of two or more separate chambers called valves. A capsule either splits into segments or opens valve tips to release its seed. Paperbarks and Bottlebrushes all produce woody capsules vital in identification.

Crimson Bottlebrush (*Callistemon citrinus*).

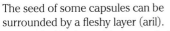

The seed of some capsules can be surrounded by a fleshy layer (aril).

Toothed Tuckeroo (*Cupaniopsis baileyana*).

The hard outer shell (hypanthium) of a Eucalyptus fruit 'Gum Nut' is part of the expanded stalk surrounding a capsule.

Blackbutt (*Eucalyptus pilularis*).

Other kinds of fruits not shown include a samara, a seed enclosed in a stiff wing, and an achene, a small dry and one-seeded fruit.

Matching samples with vegetative characteristics, preferred habitat and distribution range is the key to any conclusive plant identification.

# Index

# Further Reading

Bowmann, D.M.J.S. 2008. *Australian Rainforests*. Cambridge University Press, New York.

Brooker, M.I.H. and Kleinig, D.A. 1983. *Field Guide to Eucalypts*, Volume 1. Inkata Press Proprietary Limited, Melbourne and Sydney.

Boland, D.J., Brooker, M.I.H., Chippendale, G.M., Hall, N., Hyland, B.M.P., Kleinig, R.D., McDonald, M.W. and Tuner, J.D. 2006. *Forest Trees of Australia*. CSIRO Publishing, Melbourne.

Floyd, A.G. 2008. *Rainforest Trees of Mainland South-eastern Australia*. Terania Rainforest Publishing, Lismore, Australia.

Costermans, L. 2009. *Native Trees and Shrubs of South-Eastern Australia*. New Holland Publishers, Sydney.

Harden, G.J., McDonald, B. and Williams, J. 2006. *Rainforest Trees and Shrubs*. Gwen Harden Publishing, Nambucca, Australia

Harden, G.J. 2000. *Flora of New South Wales*, Volumes 1–4. Royal Botanical Gardens, University of NSW Press, Sydney.

Meier, L. and Figgis, P. 1985. *Rainforests of Australia*. Weldons Pty Ltd, McMahons Point, Australia.

Nickelson, N. and Nickelson, H. 1985–2004. *Rainforest Plants*, Volumes I–VI. Terania Rainforest Publishing, Lismore, Australia.

Rowell, R.J. 1991. *Ornamental Flowering Trees in Australia*. NSW University Press, Kensington, Australia

Specht, R.L. 1970. *Vegetation in the Australian Environment*. 4th edition. CSIRO Publishing/Melbourne University Press.

Webb L. J. *Classification of Australian Rain Forests*. Botany Department, University of Queensland, Brisbane.

White, M.E. 1986. *The Greening Of Gondwana*. Reed Books, Sydney.

Wrigley, J.W. and Fagg, M. 2013. *Australian Native Plants*. 6th edition. Reed New Holland, Sydney.

Wrigley, J. W. and Fagg, M. 1993. *Bottlebrushes, Paperbarks and Tea Trees*. Angus and Robertson.

# Online Resources

**Atlas of Living Australia**
http://www.ala.org.au/

**Australian Museum**
http://australianmuseum.net.au/The-geological-time-scale

**Australian National Botanic Gardens**, Australian
Plant Image Index
http://www.anbg.gov.au/cpbr/databases/index.html
http://www.anbg.gov.au/acacia/
http://www.anbg.gov.au/callistemon/

**Australia Native Plant Society**
http:www.anpsa.au

**Australian Plant Image Index**/Australian National
Herbarium
https://www.anbg.gov.au/images/photo_cd/fabaceae

**Australian Tropical Rainforest Plants
Identification Database**
www.anbg.gov.au/cpbr/cd-keys/rfk/

**Electronic Flora of South Australia**
http://www.flora.sa.gov.au
Interactive Identification Keys

**Eucalypts of Australia**
https://www.anbg.gov.au/cpbr/cd-keys/euclid3/
euclidsample/html/index.htm
https://www.anbg.gov.au/cpbr/cd-keys/euclid3/
euclidsample/html/learn.htm

**Flora of Australia Online**
http://www.environment.gov.au/biodiversity/abrs/
online-resources/flora/main/index.html
Flora of Australia Online Books, Published by ABRS,
Canberra/CSIRO, Melbourne

**FloraBase; The Western Australian Flora**
http://florabase.dpaw.wa.gov.au

**Nan and Hugh Nickelson, Rainforest Photos**
http://www.rainforestpublishing.com.au

**National Herbarium of Victoria**
http://www.rbg.vic.gov.au/

**Northern Territory Herbarium**
http://www.lrm.nt.gov.au/plants-and-animals/
herbarium

**Queensland Herbarium**
https://www.qld.gov.au/environment/plants-animals/
plants/herbarium/

**Royal Botanic Gardens, National Herbarium of
New South Wales**
http://plantnet.rbgsyd.nsw.gov.au/
http://www.rbgsyd.nsw.gov.au/education/Resources/
rainforests/Australian_Rainforests

**Tasmanian Herbarium**
http://www.tmag.tas.gov.au/collections_and_
research/tasmanian_herbarium
http://www.rbgsyd.nsw.gov.au/science/Plant_
Diversity_Research/Proteaceae_-_evolution